THE EMPEROR'S IRISH SLAVES

THE EMPEROR'S IRISH SLAVES

PRISONERS OF THE JAPANESE IN THE SECOND WORLD WAR

ROBERT WIDDERS

The
History
Press
Ireland

In caram matris meae memoriam
Sylvia May Widders
1930-1987

Dedicated to:
My niece, Jennifer Carmichael, and her beautiful daughter,
Isabelle Rose.
My niece, Danielle Tara Peet, and my great-nephews,
Oliver and Harry Peet.

First published 2012

The History Press Ireland
119 Lower Baggot Street
Dublin 2
Ireland
www.thehistorypress.ie

British Library Cataloguing in Publication Data.
A catalogue record for this book is available from the British Library.

ISBN 978 1 84588 727 8

Typesetting and origination by The History Press

CONTENTS

ACKNOWLEDGEMENTS

Many people have generously helped me during my research and I am extremely grateful to each and every one.

Harold Lock and George Simmonds are two of the dwindling band of Far East Prisoners of War – I'm indebted to them both for opening up old wounds and recounting their experiences to me. My friend, W.T.G. 'Gordon' Smale, another FEPOW, shared his experiences with me on many occasions and Sergeant Major Eric Burgoyne kindly allowed me to use material from his memoir of the British Sumatra Battalion.

Other FEPOWs, in the past, and recently, provided information for this book but chose not to be acknowledged by name, or are no longer here to be asked. Many FEPOWs preferred that their families should not know too much about their experiences. The comment, from POWs' children, or grandchildren, that, 'he only ever spoke about it in the year or so before he died' is a common one. I am most grateful to the men who spoke to me.

Thank you to the staff of the Thailand Burma Railway Centre (TBRC): Rod Beattie walked along the Death Railway with me; Andrew Snow patiently clarified various pieces of information and found references; Cliff Clegg guided me to Fusilier Kenneally's execution site. Their help has been invaluable.

The TBRC provides help and advice to anyone wishing to research a family member who worked on the Burma Railway. The museum, at Kanchanaburi, next to the Commonwealth War Graves Commission cemetery, provides a moving testament to the POWs: www.tbrconline.com.

Thank you to Tony Banham for help with issues relating to the Hong Kong POWs. His excellent book, *The Sinking of the Lisbon Maru*, gives a comprehensive account of the sinking. Anyone researching POWs captured in Hong Kong should consult Tony's website: www.hongkongwardiary.com.

I'm grateful to the Java FEPOW Club 1942 for permission to quote from *Prisoners in Java*. The club is the UK's last remaining national FEPOW veterans' association:

> Our goals are to support the remaining veterans with welfare advice and camaraderie, as well as helping researchers find out more about the FEPOW experience, so that it may be remembered, and their sacrifices honoured, for generations to come.

Associate membership is open to POWs' families and friends, and to anyone who supports the club's objectives: www.the-javafepowclub42.org.

The following people (in no particular order) generously helped me: Rod Suddaby, Margaret Martin, Lesley Clark, Jim McCorry, Kieran Coughlan, Paul Norris, Bernie McGee, Paul Cullen, Maurice O'Connell, Jonathan Moffatt, Meg Parkes, Alan Matthews, Richard Wall, Lois Mayne, Joanna Farrell, Denis Drinan, Professor G.R. Batho and Christopher Munn. If I've forgotten anyone, I apologise.

My thanks also goes to Nic, Henry, and the girls at Chickpea Cafe, Cotham Brow, Bristol, where I sat and wrote much of this book; thank you for the many excellent meals and the copious quantities of tea.

INTRODUCTION

Sister Mary Cooper, from Carrickmacross, died in a Japanese prison camp on 26 June 1943, from the combined effects of starvation, brutality, and tropical diseases. Two Irishmen, Timothy Kenneally and Patrick Fitzgerald, tried to escape from a slave labour camp on the Burma Railway and were caught, tortured, possibly crucified, and then executed on 27 March 1943. Dozens of Irish soldiers were deliberately locked in the hold of the *Lisbon Maru* when it sank on 2 October 1942: those men who managed to break out were machine-gunned in the water. Patrick Carberry, from Dublin, spent the summer of 1943 cremating the emaciated corpses of his comrades who had died from cholera. And William Perrott, from Askeaton, County Limerick, was one of a group of Irishmen who were beaten, starved, and then forced to dig their own graves before being massacred on a tropical island.

These people had two things in common: they were Irish citizens serving with the British armed forces; and they were amongst more than 650 Irish men and women who became prisoners of the Imperial Japanese Army in 1942. They suffered an incarceration marked by starvation, disease, and the denial of medical treatment. Beatings were routine, torture was commonplace, and illegal execution far from rare.

In Europe during the Second World War around 4 per cent of the Irish Prisoners of War (POW) held by Germany died in captivity. Yet by the time the Japanese POW camps were liberated in 1945, 23 per cent of the Irish POWs were dead.

The remainder – with few exceptions – were physically ill and psychologically traumatised.

Of course, as one Irish veteran made clear, in a letter written after the war to his sister in Ireland, Far East POWs (FEPOW) shared a commonality of experience regardless of nationality. Patrick Harrington, a big man, weighing thirteen stone before the war, was a seven-stone walking skeleton when he was liberated in 1945. As he told his sister, this was a result of a diet of a cup of flour boiled in water for breakfast, and two cups of watery rice, with whatever grass or weeds the cooks could find, in the evening. The desperation showed plainly in Patrick's anecdote; 'I once got the makings for seven fags from a doctor for a dead rat. He skinned and cooked an' ate it as if it was a pork chop.'[1]

Like many POWs, Patrick returned home with ulcers on his legs. We can only imagine his sister's thoughts when she heard of Patrick's fellow POWs having leg amputations without anaesthesia, because of ulcers. It must have broken this Irish girl's heart imagining her brother slaving on the Burma Railway, without boots, almost naked, starving, and being flogged when he collapsed with fatigue. But, as Harrington pointed out, this:

> was the experience of every man who was there. I do not want you to get the impression that I was any worse than anyone else, I wasn't. If you talk to any soldier who was in this Singapore show he will tell you the same story I am telling you.[2]

But this book doesn't tell the story of *all* the POWs, the men and women of many nationalities, who suffered in Japanese captivity. Neither is it a comprehensive account of every aspect of a POW's daily existence. This book has one simple aim: to give voice to the 650 Irish citizens who served with the British armed forces and became POWs of the Japanese.

After the war, the surviving POWs came home to societies that felt they had experienced enough themselves: rationing, austerity, bereavements, and the rest of the miseries that blighted the civilian population through the war years. Few people then, aside from those who experienced it, knew just how awful Japanese captivity had been. So public sympathy was necessarily limited. People wanted to move on, forget the war, and look to the future and the FEPOWs were just one more group of sufferers in an era when victims were in plentiful supply. So they did their best to get on with life, keeping the lingering effects of tropical diseases and the ticking time bomb of Post Traumatic Stress Disorder hidden behind the stiff upper lip expected of their generation. And in Southern Ireland the POWs faced the added problem of returning to a society ambivalent and sometimes hostile towards those who had travelled abroad to serve with the British Army.

Of course, not all surviving Irish FEPOWs returned to live in Ireland; some chose to live in the UK. But those who returned faced opprobrium. For the former POWs, the need for silence for security reasons was just one more added burden. Yet these are the men who fought for us in the most dreadful war in modern history. They helped defeat the three-way alliance of Nazi Germany, Fascist Italy, and militarist Japan that held the world in an iron grip of evil. It is *their* voices that I have tried to use as much as is possible here.

1

THE BACKGROUND

On 7 December 1941, Japan launched a co-ordinated series of surprise attacks on British, American, and Dutch interests in the Far East. By February 1942, Britain was defeated in Hong Kong, Singapore, and Malaya. The Dutch East Indies was in Japanese hands by March, and American resistance in the Philippines ceased with their final surrender on 6 May 1942.

The Japanese conducted a brilliantly successful military campaign, supported by overwhelming naval and air superiority: that much is incontestable. The Allied response, especially the defence of Singapore, has been the subject of controversy ever since. But a history of these campaigns, and a refutation of the myths surrounding them, is outside of the scope of this book. Suffice to say that Great Britain was fighting against Nazism and Fascism, represented by the combined might of Germany, Italy and Japan, on more fronts than it could ever have coped with. This left Britain unable to reinforce Malaya with sufficient first-line troops and lacking the air superiority that was a pre-requisite to victory in any campaign during the Second World War. In the main, Commonwealth troops and their leaders did the best they could with what they were given.

Countries involved in the combined social, industrial, economic and military endeavour of the Second World War faced similar problems. Industry had to work flat out to fulfil the demand for every type of war material from the bullet to the battleship. At the same time the reservoir of available manpower was emptied, as men of working age volunteered or were conscripted into the fighting services. The result was an acute shortage of labour. One way in which the USA and Great Britain resolved the problem, in the same way that Britain had dealt with it during the First World War, was by opening traditionally male occupations to women. The exception in Britain was mining, which was deemed too hazardous. So a proportion of British men conscripted for military service were diverted into coal mining. Immigration also helped to ease the labour shortage, as Irish men (and women), attracted by high wages in the munitions industry, travelled to England to seek work.

Japan also brought more women into industry. But immigration was not an option for them. After a decade of Japanese occupation, which had brought about the death of 15 million Chinese people, the massive pool of potential labour in nearby China had no interest in voluntary employment in Japan. And Sino-phobic Japanese attitudes, that paralleled the Nazi *untermenschen* philosophy towards Jews, precluded Chinese recruitment by inducement. So Japan came up with its own special response to the shortage of men in the internal labour market: they reintroduced slavery. And one source for this was the thousands of Allied Prisoners of War that fell into Japanese hands in 1942. This is not hyperbole. In every sense, both legal and practical, the POWs were slaves.

Under international law, it was not illegal to make POWs work. But there were strict conditions for their protection. These included the kinds of work which could be done, which excluded hazardous jobs or working in war industries. There were also minimum standards laid down for medical treatment and food. But Allied POWs were forced to work in the most dangerous areas, such as mines, whilst being denied any safety measures. They were deliberately starved and denied access to medical treatment. A savage regime of physical punishment and illegal executions was used to enforce obedience. Complaints were generally met with further punishments. Attempts to escape were met by torture and execution.

The POWs were slaves in the same sense that slaves were centuries earlier until Great Britain enforced the widespread abolition of the slave trade in the early nineteenth century. Allied soldiers became the property of the Japanese Emperor. They were held against their will, deprived of all rights, and subjected to punishments and torture. They could be killed at any time at the whim of any of their captors. But they differed in one key respect from, say, the plantation slaves two centuries earlier. Those slaves were held to have an economic value and, aside from questions of humanity, it was considered sensible to feed them and keep them alive. The POWs were deemed worthless and expendable, and they died by the thousand from starvation, brutality, preventable diseases and denial of medical treatment.

Over 132,000 servicemen and women eventually became guests of the Japanese Emperor, with the conquest of British possessions in Hong Kong and Malaya, Dutch territories in Java and Sumatra, and American colonies in Guam and the Philippines. Japan had never expected to end up with this many prisoners – their own soldiers were supposed to commit suicide rather than surrender – so their response was reactive initially and opportunistic later on.

The Japanese Army's immediate action was to gather the POWs into a number of holding centres. In some cases, such as the Bataan death march, the process was accompanied by wholesale slaughter. In the Philippines over 600 American and 5,000 Filipino soldiers were murdered during a forced march from Corregidor to Capas. Whilst in Singapore, aside from the humiliation it entailed, for most men the process was a straightforward transfer into Changi Barracks.

Japan's aims in relation to the POWs altered as the war progressed. Initially the POWs were used as a source of local labour. Then, as Allied interdiction of Japanese shipping gave impetus to plans to build a railway linking Thailand to

Burma, the POWs were seen as a strategic resource for large scale labour-intensive projects, and as a ready pool of free, expendable labour for industry. Finally, and perhaps more contentiously, in the closing months of the war, Japanese aims in relation to the POWs appear to have focused on preventing their liberation by preparing to kill them. A policy that, arguably, was only prevented from being carried out when the two atomic bombs dropped on Japan caused an immediate and unconditional Japanese surrender.

Initially, the bulk of the British POWs in Singapore were concentrated in Changi Barracks. In Hong Kong, they were held in camps at Shamshuipo and North Point. Significant numbers of British POWs were also held at camps in Java and Sumatra. Then, as the use of POW labour increased, new POW camps sprung up throughout Japanese occupied South East Asia and within Japan itself.

The Japanese POW camps eventually totalled many hundreds, located in places as diverse as jungles and industrial shipyards. So it is difficult to give any overview without resorting to generalisations. In some instances, such as at Singapore, existing prisons and barrack buildings were utilised. In Java and Sumatra a variety of former barracks, public buildings, and schools were enclosed with barbed wire and pressed into service. Camps on the Burma Railway were hacked out of the jungle by the POWs, who built their own attap huts to live in. And in places like Thailand and Burma, the jungle and the savage repercussions that followed escape attempts made barbed wire unnecessary.

Each camp was under the overall command of a Japanese officer or NCO, supported by Japanese, Korean, or Formosan guards. The camp's internal administration was the responsibility of a senior Allied officer or NCO. It was a thankless task. If the officer in charge stood up to the Japanese he would usually be savagely beaten and kicked. At the same time he would be under pressure from the POWs to intercede with the Japanese on their behalf, and accused of conspiring with the Japanese if he didn't. Most Allied officers erred on the side of duty and paid heavily for it.

The three depressingly common themes of starvation, disease, and brutality affected almost all of the POWs regardless of rank or camp location. There were exceptions of course. Men fortunate enough to be sent to one of the Japanese show camps received reasonable treatment, and were quite likely to survive the war. These camps were set up for international propaganda purposes and to hoodwink the International Red Cross (IRC). The IRC in turn sent Red Cross parcels to the POWs in South East Asia throughout the war. The Japanese Army routinely looted these, however, and on the odd occasion when they did reach the POWs, typically a parcel intended for one man would be divided between ten.

Clothing and footwear was in short supply, as fabrics and leather soon rotted in the tropics. The Fundoshi, which the troops called a 'Jap Happy',[3] became the norm, especially on the Burma Railway. This was a one-piece garment, consisting of a section of cloth tied at the waist and pulled up between the legs like a loin cloth. Footwear was in short supply and many men worked barefoot. In Japan, where the winters were brutally cold, POWs were issued with a minimum of clothing and bedding, and the flimsiest of boots. None of this was remotely adequate for the climate or the industrial working conditions of factories or coal mines.

Food was always inadequate. On the Burma Railway the official Japanese scale of rations was 2,100 calories a day for POWs.[4] This was about half the amount that was needed given the hard physical labour that the POWs did for twelve, and often many more, hours per day. But the POWs never received anything remotely near the official scale. Food was often stolen in transit. The Japanese and Korean guards looted any remaining good quality food. So the POWs were left with very little. At best, a typical meal might be some watery rice, with a tiny amount of vegetables, sometimes flavoured with dried fish. And whilst the details varied, the principle of starvation applied throughout the Japanese POW archipelago.

Punishments were savage. For instance, all POWs, regardless of rank, had to salute or bow to any Japanese or Korean guard. Failure to do so might result in being punched, slapped, beaten with a bamboo rod, being kicked senseless, or having bones broken, and on occasion men were beaten to death for not bowing properly. The punishments for more serious crimes, like operating a hidden radio, reached heights of barbarity that are hard to comprehend. A favoured Japanese torture was to hold a prisoner on the ground and fill his stomach, till visibly distended, by pouring water down his throat with a hose. Then a guard would jump on the man's stomach. A variation on this theme would be to tie barbed wire around the man's stomach before filling him with the water hose. Other favourites included being hung from a tree by the thumbs, or pulling a man's finger nails out with pliers: The list is endless ...

For attempting to escape captivity the punishment was invariably death. Sometimes men were executed by firing squad in front of their mates. Frederick Freeman recalled, 'the Japanese method; they aim at the throat – not the heart – and believe me it took several volleys to finish them off – not a nice sight I assure you.'[5]

Other means of execution, ranging from disembowelment, crucifixion, and decapitation, were also used. Men were beheaded with a Japanese officer's, or NCO's, sword. But forget any romanticised notions, from films and novels, of the Knight of Bushido's honoured blade slicing like a hot knife through butter, bringing clean and instantaneous death. Yes, in the hands of an expert it might be done that way. But the sordid reality was often an act of painful butchery, with a number of sword strokes hacking off a man's head.

That the POWs lived a life of fear, stress, and trauma is stating the obvious. They coped as best they could. What worked best for most men was to form into little groups of four or five men, sharing whatever extra food they might obtain and caring for each other when ill. Loners, lacking this powerful informal support system, tended to die first.

The Japanese, in one of the oddities of their administration, paid the POWs for their work. Of course, the cash wasn't always actually handed over. And it was only a small sum of money, and no substitute for the proper rations, clothing, medical care, and accommodation that they should have been given. In reality the wages were a sham, a device to save international face under the Geneva Convention. Depending on which camp a man was in, some of the money might be pooled and used to buy extra food for the cookhouse, or a few medicines for the sick hut. The remainder, retained on an individual basis, might be used to buy eggs, or whatever items the Japanese allowed the POWs to buy from the canteens they occasionally established. It will probably come as no surprise to hear that these prices were controlled and inflated.

Officers, who received more pay than enlisted men, could buy a little more food and had a better chance of surviving. But officers were also expected to donate some of their pay to whatever funds were established by the British camp administration, to purchase food for sick and dying men. The Japanese Army, firmly of the belief that sick POWs were a waste of resources and should be killed as soon as possible, only issued half rations to men unable to work. Sometimes they refused to issue any rations at all. This was a death sentence to starving, emaciated men suffering from injuries and disease. So, officers' donated funds were vital in helping to keep these men fed.

These fundamentals underlay everyday POW life and inform, whether stated or not, the accounts given in this book. There were a few Japanese soldiers, however, who carried out their tasks with humanity. Occasionally a Japanese civilian worker in charge of POWs displayed kindness and generosity and gave little presents of food, though they would have been severely disciplined if caught doing so. For instance, Private John Cawley, from Ballymote, reported that at Sendai No. 2 Camp, in Japan, 'the camp civilian supervisor … did much good and through the gifts of eggs and other foodstuffs … saved the lives of many people who were seriously ill.'[6]

Most British officers carried out their duties to the men under their (nominal) command conscientiously, intervening with the Japanese on their behalf, despite the temptation to take the easy route out. But there were failures, serious in some cases, of leadership too. And some enlisted men failed in their own responsibilities to the services and their comrades; theft, bullying, and racketeering were not unknown.

But if the story of the Far East POWs is complex, the actions of their captors, defies all rational comprehension at times. In some camps the Japanese would laugh at POW funeral parties carrying another corpse to a makeshift jungle cemetery. Yet on other occasions they would stand to attention and give full military honours. At Tanjong Priok, in Java, the Japanese commandant attended POW funerals and it was common for a Japanese officer to lay a wreath. But most of these deaths had been preventable, caused by deliberate starvation or denial of medical care. In the words of one British soldier, 'they are only decent to you when you are bloody well dead'.

2

MALAYA

Denis Coughlan, from Clogheen, County Tipperary, was one of the first Irish soldiers to be captured by the Japanese. He was a Lance Corporal serving with the 2nd battalion the East Surrey Regiment, in Malaya.

After the Japanese landings in Thailand and Malaya, they were moved into their assigned positions at Jitra. During the subsequent Japanese attack, over half of the East Surrey Regiment were killed or wounded. The 2nd Battalion of the Leicestershire Regiment suffered similar losses and the survivors of both battalions were joined together as a temporary composite unit designated The British Battalion.[7] Major Clive Wallis, from Dublin, became Adjutant of the new battalion. He survived the following disastrous action at Gurun and was eventually captured in Singapore.

The British Battalion was sent to hold new positions at Gurun. Japanese troops launched an early morning assault, backed up by mortars and aircraft, and the battalion's positions were over-run by infantry. Most of the senior officers and NCOs were either killed or wounded, and the remaining soldiers were dispersed and leaderless. Coughlan was one of a group of six men who hid in a paddy field, with just their heads above the water. Bandsman Austin, originally from the East Surrey Regiment, was also amongst this small group now trapped behind enemy lines.[8]

The men could either surrender or make their way back through the Japanese lines to the nearest British positions. They chose the latter option and headed south, using the sun as a compass, until they came to a village. By now they were tired, hungry, and needed help. But they didn't know what the attitude of the villagers would be, so making contact meant risking betrayal to the Japanese.

Need overcame caution and they approached an elderly Chinese lady. She told them to hide up in some nearby hills until she could arrange to bring them something to eat. True to her word, she arrived after dark with food. Then she pointed them in the right direction to avoid the Japanese troops camped nearby. This was a brave action, as the Japanese Army had quickly established a reputation for savage reprisals against anyone aiding Commonwealth soldiers.

Coughlan and the five other men headed off through the bush towards what they hoped was safety. They travelled cautiously, living off the land, eating whatever they could scavenge, and drinking coconut milk. When they arrived at the coast they found a boat and headed to Penang. They were taking a huge gamble since they didn't know if the Japanese Army had captured the island. But they hoped either to rejoin their own forces, or stock up with food and water and try to reach Sumatra.

The six men rowed over to Penang and landed there on 20 December. Tired after the row, and weakened from days of travel and lack of food, they rested on the beach. They soon found themselves facing Japanese soldiers holding rifles and bayonets. Unarmed and exhausted they had no choice but surrender.

The moment of capture, for any soldier, in any conflict, is a frightening and demoralising experience, as liberty is replaced by uncertainty and imprisonment. But becoming a prisoner of the Imperial Japanese Army brought the strong possibility of being bayoneted or shot. Luckily though, Coughlan and the others weren't killed but were imprisoned. They spent the next few weeks in Penang Jail on hard labour and short rations. Sergeant Major Albert Horrocks, of the Leicester Regiment, joined them. Horrocks, a career soldier from Dublin, was

captured off the west coast on 1 January 1942, trying to head
south by boat to rejoin his unit.

In early February the Japanese started gathering their prisoners together. They moved the men from Penang to Taiping,
about 97km to the south-east, in the state of Perak (Malaya).
When Coughlan and Horrocks arrived there, on 4 February,
they joined another Irish prisoner, Private Christopher Lynch,
from Dublin, who had also been captured on 1 January 1942.

Coughlan was transferred to Kuala Lumpur on 1 June.
Horrocks followed him a few weeks later on 30 June. They
joined up with Private Kevin Cullen, from Dublin. Cullen had
been cut off from his regiment, during the fighting retreat down
through Malaya, and trapped behind enemy lines. He had been
captured in Pontian Kechil, Southern Johore, on 2 February.

Another Dubliner, Lieutenant Clancy, 2nd battalion The
Cambridgeshire Regiment, was being held at Kuala Lumpur.
He'd been captured at Sengarang on 27 January and moved
to Kuala Lumpur on 22 February. The Cambridgeshire
Regiment, as part of 15 Brigade, had reached Sengarang early
on 26 January, but were blocked by Japanese forces holding
strong positions on the Benut Road. The surrounding ground
was thick bush and swampland, making flanking movements
difficult by foot and impossible by vehicle.

The brigade made three assaults upon the Japanese blocking
force, but was repelled each time. Eventually, they accepted that
they would not be able to get their vehicles and heavy equipment through. So the brigade commander decided to strike
out on foot through the swamp, going around the blocking
force. Clancy: 'we carried out sabotage – arms, mortars, lorries,
compasses [were] either buried or destroyed.'[9]

Whilst the brigade outflanked the Japanese on foot, the
wounded were left in the care of 198 Field Ambulance, a
Royal Army Medical Corps unit, providing first line treatment for battle casualties. Clancy had been wounded at
Sengarang, and was amongst the men left behind. He praised

the courage of the doctors, and also the Army Chaplain, Padre Duckworth, who volunteered to stay with the wounded. Clancy: '[Captain] Mark and [Captain] Welsh did wonderful work at ADS [Advanced Dressing Station] despite the attitude of the Japanese towards the wounded, I being one [of them]. All three officers' devotion to duty was outstanding.'[10]

Clancy became one of a growing band of Irish POWs in Kuala Lumpur. They were held at Pudu Gaol, which was now used by the Japanese as a centralised holding area for Commonwealth prisoners in Malaya. The gaol, built in 1895, was ill equipped for its new role. Australian soldier Russell Braddon described his arrival there:

> Huge doors opened and we passed through them. The doors closed. We were prodded into a small courtyard and that, too, was closed. Inside the courtyard we found 700 men. It had been designed to provide exercise for 30 female convicts. In it, and the cells for those 30 female convicts, we 700 were now to live, sleep, cook, excrete, wash and die.[11]

At Pudu, all rights and possessions were taken away and replaced with a routine that alternated between days of extreme boredom and backbreaking labour, punctuated by the ever constant fear of vicious beatings. Not surprisingly, everyone discussed escape. Lieutenant Clancy:

> An escape party of six officers and two ORs [other ranks] left gaol on August 13th at 2200 hours. Outside contacts had been made prior to escape. Captain MacDonald, Sergeant Bell and a sergeant from the Dutch Air Force intended making for Malacca first. Captain Hancock, Captain Nugent, Lieutenant Van Renan, Lieutenant Graham and Lieutenant Harvey went north following [the] tin mines to Kedah. Bell and the Sergeant from the Dutch Air Force were recaptured 15th August and McDonald on 31st August.

[The remainder] were recaptured after about two weeks.
Resistance was put up with Nugent being wounded.
All returned to Kuala Lumpur gaol solitary confinement.
During September all [were] taken from the gaol, put into a
lorry and tied together. [They were] believed to have been
shot somewhere in the vicinity of [the] Christian cemetery,
Kuala Lumpur.[12]

Most of the men spoke Malay and had long experience of
the country, with a network of local contacts. They were also
armed with grenades, smuggled into the jail whilst on outside
working parties, and carried supplies of food. If anyone could
have made a successful escape it was these men. But they were
betrayed to the Japanese by Malays fearful of reprisals. Some
sources disagree with Clancy over exactly when the men were
recaptured. But there is no disagreement over the fact that they
were made to dig their own graves and then executed. No one
successfully escaped from Pudu Gaol, aside from the growing
list of sick men who died for want of food and medicine.

There were also soldiers from the Argyle and Sutherland
Highlanders at Pudu. Despite being a Scottish regiment,
English and Irish soldiers served in the Argyles; C Company
was known informally as Irish Company because so many
men were of Irish origin. After the disaster at Slim River on
7 January, when Japanese tanks and motorised infantry broke
through the defensive line, many of the Argyle's surviving
soldiers were dispersed in the jungle. Some eventually got
through the Japanese lines and rejoined the British forces at
Tanjong Malim, and some escaped by sea to Sumatra. But
many died in the jungle either from disease or in skirmishes
with Japanese patrols.

One of the Irishmen serving in the Argyles, Private Grubb,
was captured around 12 January. Whilst Private Moore, from
Kilkenny, remained at large until the beginning of May when
he either handed himself in or was captured, and put in Pudu

Gaol. Jockie Bell, another Argyle and Sutherland Highlander, was probably referring to Grubb and Moore when he recalled, '... two Irish boys, they had a great job with the Japs – it was hard work carrying 2cwt bags of rice, but they got well rewarded, thieving coffee, beans, jam, cheese and MacConnochies (tinned meat) and they gave us part of their loot.'[13]

Despite the extra loot, within a period of six months, thirty-seven of the (approximately) 200 Argyle POWs in Pudu Jail died from disease and starvation.[14]

Later that year, the Japanese moved the POWs from Pudu to Singapore. Lieutenant Clancy was moved to Changi in October, where he spent the remainder of his three and a half years of captivity. Sergeant Major Horrocks and Lance Corporal Coughlan went to Singapore together on 14 October 1942. Horrocks was sent off to labour on the Burma Railway and spent the rest of the war in Thailand. Coughlan worked on the Burma Railway until 1944, when he was moved first to the Philippines and then Formosa. Finally, in 1945, after three horrendous hellship voyages, he was sent to Japan. Private Cullen left Pudu Jail in January 1943 and was sent to work on the Burma Railway in May.

3

FORCE Z

The battleship HMS *Prince of Wales*, and the battlecruiser HMS *Repulse*, escorted by four ageing destroyers, sailed from Singapore at 5.35 p.m. on 8 December 1941. Two days later, both capital ships lay on the ocean bed, accompanied by 840 members of their crews. A former Japanese staff officer, who took part in the invasion of Malaya, summed up the situation accurately saying, 'the naval action off Kuantan had annihilated in one blow the main strength of the British Far East Fleet by sinking the *Prince of Wales* and *Repulse*, and had given us complete command of the sea off the east coast of Malaya.'[15]

Force Z, which was the only naval force available for the Far East, sailed north to intercept the Japanese invasion fleet. The aircraft carrier HMS *Indomitable* had originally been allocated to provide air cover. She had, however, been damaged in the West Indies and no replacement was available. There was virtually no effective land-based air cover available from Malaya. So Force Z could sail without air cover or not at all. But sitting in harbour, whilst the Japanese Navy landed troops in Malaya, was not an option the Royal Navy was ever likely to contemplate.

At 11 a.m. on 10 December, whilst reacting to what turned out to be a false intelligence report of Japanese landings off Kuantan, HMS *Prince of Wales* and HMS *Repulse* came under a series of sustained torpedo attacks from torpedo-bombers of the Japanese Air Force. Both ships successfully evaded the first attack. At 11.44 a.m. *Repulse* turned and combed (missed) the tracks of a number of torpedoes during a second attack. But *Prince of Wales* was struck twice on the port quarter, disabling the engines. In an unlucky twist of fate, the explosion from the torpedoes knocked the shaft of one propeller from its A frame. The still revolving shaft tore a massive hole through the weakest part of the hull, causing such flooding that the damage control measures were overwhelmed and the ship started to sink.

Repeated torpedo attacks, pressed home with great courage by Japanese aircraft, in the face of intense anti-aircraft fire, eventually scored sufficient hits on *Repulse* to sink her a little after 12.30 a.m. Meanwhile, the *Prince of Wales* was settling further in the water. Her captain gave the order to abandon ship at 1.20 p.m. - she sank soon after.

A sinking ship is the story of hundreds of individual dramas, played out quickly, or at length, as the case may be. Onboard HMS *Prince of Wales* some men were able to walk on deck and calmly wait whilst taking their turn to climb across ropes thrown across from HMS *Express*, one of the accompanying destroyers. Other men remained entombed below, in magazines and watertight compartments, trapped behind armoured hatches jammed tight by twisted wreckage. Whilst in the engine and boiler rooms fractured pipes sprayed superheated steam around in a deadly spray that scalded flesh from the bone, destroying some men but missing others.

One of the stokers, Gordon Smale, told the author how he escaped unharmed from HMS *Prince of Wales'* engine room.[16] Other stokers, like John Collins, from Cork, died there. George Simmonds, a Royal Marine, recalled:

> We were helping the people out of the boiler rooms and engine rooms on to the quarterdeck and off onto the destroyers. I remember vividly I was leaning over a hatch. We were pulling men out – they'd only got singlets [vests] on because it was hot in the engine room. They'd been scalded – and as you were holding their arms to pull them up, if they slipped, their skin would peel off. That was something I don't think I'll ever forget.[17]

Able Seaman James Tobin, from County Cork, and Cook Patrick Byrne, from Wicklow, both survived the sinking of HMS *Prince of Wales*. So did two Royal Marines, Leslie Blake from Limerick and George Cleary from Dublin.

Onboard HMS *Repulse*, men jumped overboard trying to get clear of the ship as it sank. Leading Stoker Walter Ashcroft, from Ringabella, County Cork, was one of the lucky ones to emerge unscathed from the engine room. By an odd quirk of fate HMS *Repulse* also had a cook (from Dublin) onboard, called Patrick Byrne. Like his namesake on the *Prince of Wales*, he lived to get back to Singapore.

When the survivors of the two capital ships arrived in Singapore they were taken to the Fleet Shore Accommodation, fed, and given help to clean up.[18] The wounded, some of them still covered with oil, were taken to military hospitals. A lucky few amongst the survivors were sent back to the UK. But most were sent to other ships, or later manned small boats during the evacuation in the last days before Singapore capitulated.

George Simmonds, and the two Irish Marines, Blake and Cleary, became part of a composite Army and Royal Marine fighting unit. George Simmonds:

> The Marines were gathered together. We then made up two companies [and joined up] with the Argyle and Sutherland Highlanders – they'd only got two companies left after they'd fought down through Malaya. And we made up what was called the Plymouth Argyles – we were Plymouth [Royal Naval] Division 'Greens' – and, of course, they were the Argyles. After we'd been on the island [of Singapore] a short time they decided to try and get [us] behind the Jap lines. Forty of us were given very brief jungle training and we went up to join a small detachment of Argyles under [Major] Rose. But instead of getting behind their lines, they [the Japanese] moved so fast that we were outmanoeuvred and we eventually went to Port Swettenham, on the coast.

> We did some demolition work to prevent them [the Japanese] using the harbour. Then we came back to Singapore, joined the remainder of the detachment at the Fleet Shore Accommodation, and carried on until Singapore fell. [In the last couple of days prior to the capitulation] a lot of the 'Greens' [Royal Marines] that were left got away from Singapore in various small boats. And they were then caught in Java. I was still in Singapore – we were left holding the line – such as it was – while they were evacuating people by boat.[19]

Marines George Simmonds and George Cleary were captured at Singapore. Marine Leslie Blake was captured in the Banka Straits on 14 February, as was Patrick Byrne (HMS *Repulse*). They'd escaped on one of the many small boats that left Singapore in the last couple of days before the garrison surrendered. Walter Ashcroft and James Tobin were captured in the same place the following day.

Stoker Smale had been sent to two other small ships which were both sunk in action against the Japanese. Then, along with some other former *Prince of Wales* crew, he was sent to evacuate European residents from an island. After they'd got the civilians to the mainland, he recalled, 'Our officer ran off and left us. When we got back to Singapore we were all "heroes" and all that for getting the civilians out. But then the officer turned up and said that we were the ones who had got windy. I was court-martialled – I got my revenge in the end though.'[20]

Smale escaped from Singapore, but was eventually captured in Sumatra on 17 March, 'I volunteered to stay behind and help man one of the escape lines, that's why I was bloody caught.'[21] Patrick Byrne (HMS *Prince of Wales*) was caught there too, though whether or not he was involved in manning the escape lines isn't known. The escape line had been set up by a Royal Marine, Lieutenant Colonel Alan Warren. He'd pressured the authorities to allow him to form an official escape route, and stocked a string of small islands, from Singapore to Moro Island, with supplies. An operational base was set up on the Sumatran coast, near Priggi Rajah, and escapees who made it this far were sent down the Indragiri River in boats. These boats were manned by men from his escape organisation, plus escapees who volunteered to take a turn helping. From there onwards escapees were sent by train to Padang and evacuated to Ceylon.

Men like Gordon Smale, who volunteered to stay behind to man the escape line, gave up their own chance to reach safety in order to help others. One of the many Irishmen who travelled along this route was Thomas Walsh, from Tipperary. Walsh was a Gunner in 9th Coast Regiment, Royal Artillery. Walsh:

> On 16th February 1942, I left Palua Tekong off Singapore with 14 other men of 22 Coast Battery, 9th Coast Regiment, in a motor launch. We picked up forty survivors of a ship from an island – thirty women nurses – European and Eurasian – and ten male Australians [soldiers]. We left them at their request at Palau D ... and then proceeded to [Padang] Sumatra.[22]

This may have been the boat under the command of Captain James Gordon, 22nd Coast battery:

> I took a small craft with a motor ... from Tekong Island ... and with some hazards reached the Indragiri River, Sumatra.[23]

After this the group split up, some stayed to help, running the escape line, and some proceeding along it to Padang.

Michael Hunt, another Irish gunner: '[I] escaped from Singapore to Sumatra on 16 February 1942.'[24] The Dutch authorities in Sumatra aided Commonwealth soldiers that made it as far as Padang, and many Dutch civilians were generous in feeding and sheltering escapees. However, the Dutch civil authorities were well aware that it was only a question of time before the island came under Japanese occupation. And their main concern was ensuring a peaceful handover, with minimal casualties.

The last British and Australian rescue ships took off as many men as they could. The men who were left behind became increasingly desperate and tried to buy, borrow, or steal any local craft that could float. Some of those who managed to find a small boat eventually made it to Ceylon, though most either died at sea or were captured by the Japanese Navy. But it was a soldier's duty to try to escape and return to continue fighting, though the Dutch civil authorities in Sumatra eventually hindered this. Michael Hunt: 'We were disarmed by the Dutch and anybody who went down to the docks to try and get a boat was stopped by the Dutch police.'[25]

The Dutch authorities insisted on keeping a number of ships in the harbour. They imagined the Japanese would allow them to use these to continue with trade and administrative duties after they took over. This infuriated many of the Commonwealth servicemen still keen to make an escape, and attempts were made to seize the vessels. So the Dutch put the ships under armed guard.

The majority of servicemen left in Padang were disciplined and motivated. However, a small number of men, who had deserted from Singapore before the capitulation, were stealing food from the local populace. The situation was eventually brought under control by British officers, led by Lieutenant Colonel Warren.

With many of the soldiers lacking weapons, and burdened by large numbers of wounded men, there was no hope of resistance when the Japanese arrived at Padang. Captain Gordon: 'I surrendered, under [the command of] Lieutenant Colonel Warren RM, to Japanese forces on their entering Padang on 17 March 1942, along with 1,100 British officers and men awaiting evacuation.'[26] The Japanese decided to form a large work party from these men. The Senior British Officer (SBO) was ordered to select 500 men from the 1,000 plus Army, Navy, and RAF POWs. At least five Irishmen were included in the battalion: Patrick Byrne, Michael Hunt, Desmond Cusack, Thomas Walsh and Richard Beatty.

Captain Dudley Apthorpe, an officer in the Royal Artillery, was appointed to command this newly formed British Sumatra Battalion. And Sergeant Eric Burgoyne was appointed senior Battalion Sergeant Major. Starvation rations and imprisonment were already taking a toll on the physical and mental health of the POWs. To make matters worse, a small number of men were hard cases and troublemakers, included by the SBO in order to get rid of them and pass the problem onto someone else.

Both Apthorpe and Burgoyne recognised the importance of maintaining discipline to ensure co-operative survival. As they readied to march out of Padang, on 9 April 1942, Captain Apthorpe spoke to the assembled parade. He told them what little he knew about whatever hell the Japanese planned for them all. Then Battery Sergeant Major Burgoyne, keen to re-build the men's *esprit de corps*, addressed the battalion.

They stood on the parade ground of the former Dutch barracks used to house the POWs. The officers were fallen in on one side, and the 479 nine other ranks stood opposite. Burgoyne silently contemplated the words spoken by the Japanese Commandant a few days earlier. He'd said, 'you men are the tattered remnants of a degenerate nation – The Japanese Emperor has seen fit to spare your lives for work on the noble project of railway building – Thousands of you will die and leave your bones to bleach on the lines'.

Then Burgoyne spoke to the ranks of POWs. He told them that whilst they may well be tattered, bootless, and in some cases nearly naked, it was something to be proud of rather than ashamed. The reason that many of them were there was because of the sacrifice they made rescuing and helping others to escape.[27] He also reminded them that it was only by maintaining discipline, and remaining servicemen, that they had any hope of survival. And this straightforward axiom – to which must be added good leadership – made the difference between survival and decimation, and formed the bedrock of the best Allied units.

Finally, Sergeant Major Burgoyne asked them to march out of camp with their heads held high whistling the tune of Colonel Bogey.[28] And that is just what they did. These tattered, starving, battered men, a few even carried on stretchers, lifted their heads high and marched off singing. Some whistled the tune and others sang the words (though not quite the version the Japanese expected); 'Bollocks, and the same to you'.

The British Sumatra Battalion was then shipped to Burma to build the Burma section of the Japanese death railway. They started work in October 1942. Their first camp was Helpauk, otherwise known as 18 Kilo Camp as it was 18km from the starting point. As with most camps on the railway it had to be built by the prisoners, from bamboo and attap, using a minimum of tools to produce rudimentary huts to sleep in.

After a couple of weeks the Japanese guards were replaced by Koreans. According to Gordon Smale:

The Koreans were even worse than the Japs. We had to learn to number off in Japanese – which a lot of the lads found hard going – so no one wanted to be in the front rank when we paraded in the morning to be counted by the guards and sent to work. *Ichi, ni, san, shi* … and if you got the counting in Japanese wrong you'd get a bashing. I was really tall and the Japs didn't like tall people and sometimes they'd beat you up just for being tall. But also I was young and baby faced and they sometimes went a bit easier on really young fellas. So they never used to know whether to beat me up or let me off.[29]

Food was always distributed fairly with equal shares for all. An obvious thing to do one might say. But when you are literally starving to death, and suffering the painful effects of vitamin deficiency diseases, the temptation to fiddle, to steal, to do anything to survive, even at the expense of your comrades' lives, can be almost overwhelmingly tempting. Food remained the focal point of POW survival. Smale:

> I would eat anything. We had a Dutch doctor with us in one camp and he knew which plants you could eat and which ones could be used in place of medicines and all that. And if you wanted to get through it you just had to eat absolutely anything and not be squeamish. But some men just couldn't face some of the worst filth we had to eat and they were the ones who died first.[30]

The British Sumatra Battalion progressed south along the railway from work camp to work camp. Captain Apthorpe became deeply respected by his men for constantly intervening on their behalf and standing between them and the Japanese. But despite the best efforts of the commanding officer, the medical staff, and the men themselves, they trailed a wake of dead servicemen behind them.

Of course, it's an officer's duty to care for the welfare of the men under his command – even whilst in captivity. But it wasn't an easy duty to carry out. Some officers on the Railway were executed for standing up for their men, and savage beatings were common for officers who spoke out. On one occasion Apthorpe was called upon by the Japanese to account for something that his men had done. He couldn't understand what was being said and the Japanese beat him to the ground. When he stood up he 'told them to stop shouting in their monkey language and to go and get an interpreter'. For this he was made to stand in the blazing tropical heat all day holding a boulder over his head. Whenever he fainted, from exhaustion and dehydration, he had water thrown over him to revive him and was then beaten to his feet and made to continue with the punishment.

This sort of punishment and others far worse, was common-place. It took a special kind of courage, different to that needed in the heat of battle, to confront the Japanese day-in-day-out, for months, and years, knowing that every time you spoke you might be badly beaten. Captain Apthorpe had this quality, though not all officers did.

As the British Sumatra Battalion continued along the railway, the already dire food situation worsened. This was a routine experience for all Allied units, regardless of whether they started from the Burmese or Thai end of the railway. As they moved further from the food depots it became more dif-ficult to supply food up country, due to the distances involved and the difficult terrain. The situation was exacerbated during the monsoon season, when torrential rain made progress along dirt roads and swollen rivers nearly impossible.

The battalion reached 114 Kilo Camp by the beginning of November 1943. At this point they had suffered eighty-six deaths. Some men had been left in camps in Burma and fifty men had been left at 55 Kilo Camp, too sick, even by Japanese reckoning, to work anymore. Their much-respected Australian medical officer, Lieutenant Colonel Coates, stayed there with them. Most of the remainder of the battalion, numbering about 300, were sent in cattle trucks to Kanburi camp and base hospital in January 1944. Of course, this wasn't a hospital by the standards that we would recognise now. But conditions at Kanburi were better than they'd experienced previously, with slightly more food available, and the death rate decreased.

In March the battalion was split up with some men detached to join 51 Kumi, a work party sent to Saigon. Michael Hunt was amongst the men sent to Saigon, where he stayed for the remainder of the war. Smale, and the four Irishmen, Byrne, Cusack, Walsh, and Beatty, remained with the rest of the bat-talion in Thailand.

Desmond Cusack spent some time at Nakom Pathon camp. The camp also held loyal soldiers from the Indian Army who had resisted all threats and inducements and refused to join the Japanese sponsored Indian National Army. Thousands of Indian soldiers had been captured when Singapore capitulated. Many were genuinely keen to join the new force under the command of Mohan Singh. Some, whilst having little interest in its aims, saw an opportunity to avoid imprisonment. Others, despite seeing comrades beaten and even executed, refused to bow to Japanese threats. And, of course, the Ghurkhas refused to a man. All of them paid a heavy price for their courage and loyalty.

Cusack joined some British and Australian soldiers at Nakom Pathon who had formed a small singing group. With the war going against them, and work on the Railway completed, the Japanese relented a little and allowed the POWs a few simple entertainments. Len Gibson, a British soldier, was also in the group. Gibson:

> The Japanese did not allow any contact between us [the British POWs] and those gallant Indians, but seven of us managed to get inside their compound … [including] Paddy Cusack a great Irish lad … [we] were very fond of singing in harmony. We practised together and called ourselves, '5 boys and 6 strings'.[31]

Whilst the Japanese always kept the Indian soldiers separated from the British POWs, they were persuaded that allowing the Indians to listen to the singing group would cause no harm. So Gibson, Cusack, and the rest of the group, went into the Indian compound, accompanied by a Japanese guard. They also had an extra member of the group who, unknown to the Japanese, was a (British) officer in the Indian Army. He sat next to one of the senior Indian officers and exchanged information about camp conditions and shared plans for when the camps were finally liberated.

Gordon Smale, and the four Irishmen, Pat Byrne, Desmond Cusack, Thomas Walsh, and Richard Beatty, survived captivity and returned home after the war. Both Smale and Byrne remained in the Royal Navy and had long and distinguished careers. Byrne retired in 1966 and returned to Wicklow, Ireland.

5

JAVA

In the last few weeks before Singapore surrendered, some of the British reinforcements were diverted to Java, in the Dutch East Indies. Their task was to block the Japanese advance upon Australia. The remaining RAF aircraft defending Malaya and Singapore were also moved there, along with evacuated personnel from all three services, many of them technicians and non combatants, such as medical personnel.

The Japanese Army landed on the west coast of Java on 28 February 1942, and on 8 March the Dutch Army surrendered the island to the Japanese. Thousands of British servicemen went into captivity, amongst them a number of RAF aircrew. One of them – determined to evade capture – was Sergeant Peter Ryan, from Cork.

Ryan was a pilot serving with 232 Squadron RAF. The squadron left England in November 1941, destined for the Middle East. By the time the convoy arrived in South Africa, Japan had launched its surprise attacks and 232 Squadron was diverted to Singapore. The ground crews disembarked at Singapore on 13 January 1942. The squadron's pilots, embarked on the aircraft carrier HMS *Indomitable*, flew off to Java on 27 January, as the Singapore airfields were untenable due to Japanese bombing. The pilots were reunited with the ground crews at Palembang, in Sumatra, on 2 February. However, the Japanese landings forced a withdrawal to Java on 15 February.

Many of 232 Squadron's ground echelon were evacuated to Ceylon. Most of the squadron's aircraft had been destroyed by now and the surviving pilots, including Ryan, were in transit at

Garoet (Java) awaiting transport to Colombo. On the evening of 7 March, Ryan was told that the Dutch Army intended to capitulate and, that, 'we should lay down our arms and await capture by the Japanese but that if we felt inclined, we could make an attempt to escape.'[32]

Most of the pilots decided to make for the coast to look for a boat, or try to find a serviceable aircraft at another airfield. A party of around fifteen British, Australian, and Canadian pilots, and one Eurasian RAF Technician, immediately left Garoet. They travelled overnight and arrived early the following morning at a small airfield, called Tjilatjap, on the southern coast. Ryan:

> We went to the control tower and met a Dutch air force officer and his wife, and a Dutch civilian. They ... were in radio contact with a Catalina flying boat which was based on the lake at Garoet. The Dutch officer informed the Catalina of our situation and it was confirmed that they would land on the bay and fly us out to Australia. Shortly afterwards the Catalina made a recce but returned to base. We were instructed to put out a wind direction sign on the beach and the Catalina was to land in thirty minutes and pick us up.[33]

The excitement and tension that the men must have felt, believing rescue and escape was imminent, is unimaginable. Their disappointment at what followed must have been all the greater because of it.

> Within half an hour, the Catalina appeared overhead but did not land ... I heard later that the British crew of the plane were ordered to hand over the Catalina by the Dutch and this order was enforced at the point of a gun.[34]

The men then worked to fill in some of the craters blown in the runway by a Dutch Army officer, and repaired one of two Lockheed aircraft they had found. The aircraft, piloted by the

Dutch officer they had met in the control tower, took off with five of the British and Canadian pilots, and eventually reached Australia. Ryan and the other men tried, unsuccessfully, to repair the remaining aircraft. Ryan:

> We decided to move into the jungle and hide out. We remained hiding for another six weeks and during this time attempted to launch a small boat which we had built with the help of the natives. But this was destroyed in the surf. Towards the end of April '42, most of the party were suffering from lack of food, exposure and malaria.[35]

The men had done everything humanly possible to escape. But, as they grew increasingly ill and hungry, it was clear that they would eventually all die where they hid. So the group split into smaller parties, made their way to POW camps, and handed themselves in. Ryan surrendered to the Japanese at Bandoeng and was placed in the prison hospital for a few weeks. Then he was sent to work on an airfield construction site in Sumatra. In June 1945 he was sent to Changi Jail, Singapore, and placed in the hospital until liberation at the end of the war.

Wing Commander Harold Maguire, from County Clare, was also captured on Java. He was a Hurricane fighter pilot flying one of the handful of modern aircraft rushed out to the Far East. Their Hurricanes had been intended for operations in the deserts of North Africa, with long-range fuel tanks and special air filters. This reduced their flying capabilities and put them at a distinct disadvantage against Japanese fighters. Nonetheless, Maguire and the other pilots took them up against the numerically superior Japanese air force on a daily basis.

As the aeroplanes were destroyed, the RAF found itself with more pilots than aircraft. Ideally they would have been evacuated to India or Ceylon to fight again as they knew best, in the air. This wasn't possible and many of them went into captivity in Java. However, when captured, RAF pilots were expected to attempt to escape.

In the initial stages of captivity escape committees were formed in most camps. Maguire was on the Escape Committee in his first two camps, Glodok Prison, and Tandjong Priok, in Batavia. Soon after Maguire's tenure commenced, there was an escape attempt at Glodok, though whether it was officially backed by the Escape Committee isn't known. Maguire: 'In April 1942 P/O Siddell, Sgt Smith, and Sgt Wilson (Canadian) of 57 Squadron RAF attempted to escape ... they were caught on the aerodrome at Kemajoram and shot.'[36] The only witnesses to this execution were some Javanese civilians who showed the location of the graves to Squadron Leader Giles (Dublin) after the war.

Maguire was a married man. Like every other serviceman captured by the Japanese, married or not, he had a family at home who didn't know if he was alive or dead. Those men who escaped prior to the capitulation were interviewed in an attempt to establish casualty figures. And the International Red Cross served the role of go-between in all theatres of war, exchanging information between respective governments about POWs. But the effectiveness of this depended on the co-operation of the holding power, and with Japan this co-operation was not always forthcoming.

So it took a long time to establish exactly who had died and who was a POW in the Far East. Maguire's wife received a telegram informing her that her husband was missing. This was confirmed in a letter from the Air Council:

> ... your husband Wing Commander Maguire, Royal Air Force, is missing but is believed to have been taken prisoner of war. Your husband was in Java and unhappily there is no evidence that he had left the island when it was finally occupied by the enemy ... as soon as any definite news is received it will be at once communicated to you.[37]

The newspapers contained long columns of 'Missing' advertisements with appeals for information. Mrs Maguire posted an advert in the restrained tones common to these appeals: 'MAGUIRE. Reported missing in Java, believed prisoner of war. Wing Commander H.J. Maguire. Any information gratefully received by his wife …' Mrs Maguire eventually discovered that her husband was being held as a POW, though there were many families who didn't know if their relative had been killed or captured until after the war.

POWs were sometimes allowed to send postcards home and families could write letters in response. This was done via the International Red Cross, though in practice the despatch and receipt of mail depended on the whims of the Japanese Army camp commanders. Maguire sent a number of POW postcards home to his wife. Postcards were usually pre-printed, with the option to choose from a number of phrases, such as 'I am well/I am unwell' and so on.

Maguire was able to write a message on his cards. One of the three cards he sent during his three and a half years captivity arrived in Dublin in July 1945, during the closing stages of the war. It had the almost obligatory POW declaration of good health, added out of concern for families and to placate the Japanese who wouldn't allow anything critical to be sent:

> My darling, I am now in a Japanese Prisoner of War camp in Java. I am constantly thinking of you. It will be wonderful when we meet again. My health is excellent. Kenneth is growing up, nearly three. Many happy returns to him, and you. Hope to be with you next birthday.[38]

Sometimes POW postcards took a year or more in transit, if they arrived at all. It was not uncommon for families to have the distressing experience of reading a 'love and best wishes' message from a long dead son or brother. However, POWs' incoming post had the greatest potential for emotional disaster. Any serviceman will tell you that during wartime one of the most important things in his life is mail from home. And POWs in Japanese hands, starving, sick, and bereft of anything much in the way of comfort, positively ached for news from home.

The Japanese camp administration often used the threat of withholding mail to blackmail POWs into greater efforts at work. Occasionally mail was burnt or withheld without reason. Despite this, some mail did get through to individual POWs. Sometimes a letter, usually shared with mates, inspired a man to fight to stay alive, rekindling dreams of home. But letters also held bad news, like the death of a soldier's mother, or discovering that the fiancé a man had spent the last two years dreaming about had got married.

Squadron Leader Aidan MacCarthy (Cork), as Senior British Officer at his camp in Japan, was concerned about the potentially lethal effect of news from home. None of the men who had accompanied him from Java to Japan received letters prior to 1944 and 60 per cent of the intended recipients had died by the time the first delivery of mail arrived. For the remainder, receiving mail proved disastrous. MacCarthy:

> Even the most out of date news from home was far too great an emotional experience for us all. We were considerably debilitated and found each day a battle for survival. A further drop in morale resulted. Lethargic and unmindful of beatings the men ... had lost the will to live.[39]

The effect on those who didn't receive mail was just as grim, as men imagined themselves forgotten. Mail deliveries seemed to produce lethal consequences, whether a man received a letter or not. And MacCarthy, in agreement with the senior officers commanding other nationalities, didn't issue the other two deliveries the camp received and secretly burnt the letters.

5

FATHER GILES

Some 200 British combatant arm servicemen – mostly soldiers – took to the hills and continued fighting after the Dutch
military surrender of Java. Eventually they were captured,
and then tortured by the Kempeitai. The subsequent massacre was described by over sixty eye witnesses at The Hague
(Netherlands) after the war. Each man was crammed inside a
small bamboo pig basket. They were transported in trucks to
the coast and then put onboard ships and taken out to sea. The
baskets containing the POWs were thrown overboard. Every
man was either drowned or eaten alive by sharks.

Squadron Leader (Padre) Alan Giles, from Dublin, was
trapped on Java when the Japanese Army over-ran the island.
Flying Officer Sid Scales recalled seeing Giles at Tasik Malaya
aerodrome. The original intention was that the airmen
would be armed, and then take to the hills and fight on as
infantry. Most of the RAF men were pilots, mechanics, and
aircraft tradesmen, with little military (infantry) training, and
were probably relieved when the plan changed. Scales: 'the
fight was cancelled … and we finished up with all the others
on Tasik aerodrome … [where] in one corner [of a hangar]
was a clutch of … padres comfortably ensconced in their
sanctuary; the name Padre Giles springs to mind.'[40] Squadron
Leader Giles:

> I left Singapore the day before it fell and went to Java. I vis-
> ited what units there were and then we were sent up into
> the hills to fight. We were organised into two bodies but on

8th March after the Dutch capitulated we were ordered to Tasik Malaya. The Japs arrived about ten days after this.[41]

Initially they were guarded by front-line (combat) troops. These were replaced by Japanese and Korean second echelon guards, who immediately tightened discipline and instigated a brutal punishment regime. Giles:

> The [POW] camp leader at Tasik Malaya, Wing Commander Steedman, set the tone for the whole camp. He steadfastly refused to 'play' with the Japanese and held out courageously on our behalf, knowing ultimately what would happen … eventually he was taken out to the aerodrome and shot.[42]

All British aircrew had been ordered to fill out a questionnaire giving information about Allied aircrew training methods. According to Squadron Leader Aidan MacCarthy (from Cork):

> [Wing Commander Steedman] refused to allow these forms to be completed. He was taken to the guardroom and beaten up. After the assembly bell had been sounded, he was paraded in front of us and we then witnessed his death by firing squad. It was a horrific moment.[43]

Perhaps Wing Commander Steedman's murder inspired revenge, as there was a serious incidence of sabotage. Giles: 'A party of men working at Tasik Malaya aerodrome blocked all the drains that were installed under the runway. They were then moved, fortunately before the Japs discovered this, as during the first rains the whole of the runway was washed away.'[44]

There were a number of escape attempts at Tasik Malaya. Leading Aircraftsman Leslie Sheerin, from Dublin, joined a group of officers and airmen who had come up with a bold plan. They commandeered a lorry, loaded it with timber and tools and drove off openly, fooling the Japanese into thinking that they had been sent to repair a damaged bridge at Simpang. Eventually they reached Tjipatoedjah, on the coast. They were there for around six weeks, trying to buy or build a boat, until they were caught. But they did have one unusual stroke of luck. Re-captured escapees were invariably tortured and then executed: yet the Japanese occasionally surprised everyone. Flying Officer Scales:

> The Nips came down and picked us up at their leisure. They knew we couldn't get away and the local natives had been letting them know all about us for a small reward. We were lucky to be taken by a Jap sergeant and his unit who thought it was a fine joke that we had been trying to build a boat. He spoke very good English … he was a Tokyo University graduate. Taking a cue from their sergeant, the Nips produced cigarettes and iced drinks and treated us like humans.[45]

Sheerin was eventually taken to a small POW camp in a school at Garoet and later moved to Singapore. He died on 24 June 1944 *en route* to Japan onboard the *Tamahoko Maru*, which was sunk in Nagasaki Bay. Squadron Leader Giles was moved from Tasik Malaya to Lyceum camp, in Surabaya, a former school. After being interrogated, Giles was allowed to write a *pro forma* postcard to his family saying he was being well treated, though the postcard never arrived.

Between April and May 1943 Giles undertook the duties of Padre at Tjimahi. This was a former Dutch military barracks, now used as a POW camp. Giles' task was not easy as the Japanese were suspicious of any organised activities, especially those of a religious nature. An airman imprisoned there described some of the problems:

> While at Tjimahi, a church service (a rare event) was to be held. Most bibles and hymn books had disappeared, as the

paper pages was substituted for cigarette papers or used as currency by non-smokers [to exchange for some other item with a smoker]. Padre Alan Giles, formerly of [RAF] Selatar, therefore wrote the words of the chosen hymn on the blackboard. Unfortunately, a Japanese [guard], with some knowledge of English, inspected the room prior to the service and read the message 'Onward Christian Soldiers, marching as to war'. The minister was interrogated by the Kempeitai (the Japanese Gestapo), presumably for inciting the troops to take up arms and the church service was cancelled … [and] to my knowledge no church services were ever held [at Tjimahi] during those POW days.[46]

Like many other POWs, Giles was moved between a number of different camps in Batavia and Bandoeng. After the war he described Japanese war crimes whilst being de-briefed:

There were attempted escapes from Batavia Jail [POW Camp]. Three men got away and reached the civil airport and seized an aircraft but were captured by the Japs before they could take off. They were subsequently beaten up and shot, and their graves have been found on the perimeter of the aerodrome in Batavia.[47]

Squadron Leader Giles survived captivity. After the war he was transferred to Singapore and posted home, via Liverpool, onboard the MV *Cilicia*.

6

KIERAN CONNOLLY AND WILLIAM KENNEALLY

Sergeant Kieran Connolly, from Longford, was an RAF Wireless Operator/Air Gunner with 100 Squadron RAF. They were based at Selatar airfield (in Singapore) when the Japanese Army invaded Malaya. Apart from one flight re-equipped with modern Beaufort medium bombers, the squadron flew obsolete Vildebeest bombers. These were so slow that they were considered too vulnerable to use in daylight attacks and were held in reserve to defend Singapore against seaborne assault.

Connolly's war started at around 4 a.m. on 8 December 1941, during the first Japanese air raid on Singapore, when bombs fell on Selatar. The squadron was then transferred to Kuantan, in Malaya, where one aircraft was lost on the ground during a Japanese air raid on 10 December. During the rest of December, 100 Squadron made a number of night attacks on Japanese forces, as they advanced through Malaya. The squadron then withdrew to Singapore and on 20 January 1942 they destroyed six Japanese aircraft now at their former base in Kuantan.

On 25 January the crews took part in another bombing mission against Japanese troop concentrations and transport in central Johore, Malaya. The crews returned to base, tired after their mission, to learn that another Japanese invasion force was landing at Endau, on the east coast of Malaya. This consisted of two cruisers, twelve destroyers and two troop transports, supported by plentiful air cover from the Japanese Air Force armed with the most up-to-date fighter aircraft in the Far East. Their task was to attack this force in a daylight raid. This would prove to be 100 Squadron's greatest challenge, in an already tough campaign, for which their aircraft were totally inadequate.

The crews knew that going up against this naval task force, in their lumbering un-armoured biplanes, was likely to be a one-way trip. Wing Commander Alan Giles, a priest from Dublin, was the Padre at RAF Selatar. He witnessed the planes take off:

> I saw the Squadron setting out on that last raid on Endau. Their actions were more than the ordinary fulfilment of duty; for flying Vildebeest aircraft on a daylight raid, they knew they had little chance of coming through unscathed. As I spoke to a good many of them before they set off, I knew a good deal of their feelings; their gallantry, there-fore, to me, is a very real thing.[48]

A combined force (from 100 and 36 Squadrons) consisting of twenty-one Vildebeest bombers, three Albacores, and nine more modern Hudson bombers, attacked in two waves, a couple of hours apart. They were supported by an escort of fifteen Buffalos, an outdated fighter totally outmatched by all Japanese fighter aircraft, plus eight Hurricanes hastily diverted from the Middle East and still equipped for a ground attack role.

Sergeant Connolly took part in the first of the two raids on Endau. He was the Wireless Operator/Air Gunner in a Vildebeest, piloted by Flying Officer Reggie Lamb. Lamb's aircraft was on the starboard side of the lead section as they approached the Japanese invasion force. The shallow waters near Endau were not deep enough for air-dropped torpe-does to arm themselves so they attacked using conventional bombs. As they emerged from the cloud cover and closed with the targets, the slow-moving aircraft were an easy target for the Japanese naval AA guns and the supporting Zero fighters. Despite this, the crews pressed home their attack and managed to score a few hits on the transports.

The bomb release mechanism on Connolly's aircraft jammed and they were unable to drop their bomb load. So Lamb headed south along the coast, following the line of the Mersing Road, pursued by a Japanese fighter which he managed to evade. Over half of the RAF bombers were shot down, crashing into the sea or into the jungle along the coastline. Some of the aircrew who parachuted out of their aircraft or survived crash landings escaped back to Singapore. A few were captured by Japanese soldiers and executed. Most of the aircraft that made it back to Singapore were damaged and many of their crews were wounded.

The remaining aircraft from 100 Squadron were withdrawn to Java on 8 February, and combined with 36 Squadron. Connolly wasn't included on the combined squadron strength. It isn't clear if this is because he was wounded at Endau or because there were insufficient aircraft for the available aircrew. But at some stage he was evacuated from (probably) Java, and sent to Australia in one of the ships that successfully escaped prior to the capitulation.

Connolly may have escaped on the *Tung Song*, a small cargo ship requisitioned in December 1939 as an RAF Auxiliary Vessel. The *Tung Song* left Tjilatjap in Java on 2 March and arrived in Freemantle on 12 March. Or he may have escaped on the *Empire Star*, which carried around 2,000 RAF and Naval personnel plus 135 Australian deserters who forced their way onboard at gunpoint, arriving (via Tanjong Priok, Java) in Freemantle in March. Regardless, Connolly did escape and reached Australia and in June 1942 he sailed as a passenger onboard the SS *Hauraki*, a New Zealand registered cargo vessel, bound for Egypt. In a grim stroke of bad luck the *Hauraki* was intercepted on 12 July by two Japanese Armed Merchant Cruisers, the *Aikoku Maru*, and the *Hokuku Maru*, raiding deep into the Indian Ocean.

Connolly was taken prisoner along with the other passengers and crew. A Japanese prize crew sailed the ship to Penang and Connolly was transferred to a POW camp in Singapore. His sojourn in Singapore was a brief one. In November 1942 he was sent up to Thailand, under the command of Lieutenant Colonel Swinton, of the East Surrey Regiment, to work on the Burma Railway.

After the war Edwin Loughlin, Connolly's friend, wrote to his sister in Ireland:

> Paddy and I were together most of the time on that Railway … except for some pretty severe attacks of malaria now and again he managed to keep remarkably fit. When we were sent to different camps he had put on weight and looked more cheerful and healthier than I had ever seen him before.
>
> Paddy was the bravest fellow I ever knew. He did not seem to understand what fear meant and was continually doing the most dangerous things that could have got him shot a dozen times. I used to try to restrain him from time to time, but all I could get was a grin and a Malayan expression of which he was fond; 'Teed apa'; It means 'nothing matters'. He used to break out of the camp at night to go off into the jungle and trade with the Thais, so as to bring in food and money to the camp for his friends and some of the sick.[49]

Trading with the Thais provided a few illicitly gained medicines that saved lives in the camp hospitals on the Railway. However, the Japanese readily executed men caught trading. Loughlin: '[Paddy] used to talk to me so much about his home and about all of you, about your father and your mother, about you … about your horses and his adventures as a boy [in Ireland].' Then Loughlin apologised that, 'I can tell you nothing of the circumstances of his death – when or where he died.'[50]

Kieran Connolly's health was finally broken by starvation, overwork, and disease. He died of amoebic dysentery at Tha Rua, on 12 August 1945. After the war he was honoured with a posthumous mention in Dispatches, 'in recognition of gallant and distinguished service whilst a prisoner of war in Japanese hands'.

Connolly wasn't the only Irishman seized in a merchant ship at sea. William Kenneally, a merchant seaman, from Youghal, County Cork, fell into Japanese hands after the SS *Wellpark* was captured in the South Atlantic. A German commerce raider, the *Thor*, intercepted the *Wellpark* on 29 April 1942. *Thor* looked like an ordinary merchant ship but was armed with three hidden 6-inch guns – weapons of the same calibre that might be found on a light cruiser.

Two days later *Wellpark*'s captured seamen were joined by the crew of another British merchantman, the *Willesden*. The wounded from both captured crews were given medical attention. The remainder were also treated decently by the Germans; they were well fed and allowed to exercise on deck for an hour every day.

On 4 May all the captured seamen were transferred to the *Regensburg*, a German supply ship. They were onboard the *Regensberg* for over a month.[51] There were around 450 captured seamen onboard. Again, they were well treated and allowed out of their guarded quarters to exercise. The *Regensburg's* Captain had been a POW of the British during the First World War, which probably explained his actions.

The *Regensberg* anchored in Yokohama Harbour on 13 July and the prisoners were transferred to yet another German ship, the *Ramses*. Despite being allies, there was a good deal of mutual mistrust and even dislike between the Germans and the Japanese, on both an individual and governmental level. The captured British seamen – who were civilians – had been told they would be taken to Germany and interned there.

Unfortunately Germany and Japan reached an agreement over the handling of captured seaman, which meant that the captain of the *Ramses* had no choice but to hand over the captives to the Japanese. The prisoners were sent ashore under guard on 25 August, carrying the sacks of food given them by the German crew and were handed into Japanese custody. Many of the civilian prisoners, including some women and children, were taken to a former monastery at Fukushima, around 200 miles north of Tokyo.

Kenneally was put amongst the military POWs. These men were put into open lorries and driven around Yokohama, whilst being bombarded with stones and the filth the local civilians picked up from the gutters to use as missiles. Many of the seamen, including Kenneally, finally ended up in Kawasaki Camp (Tokyo) where they remained until liberation in 1945.

Though he would have struggled to see it this way at the time, Kenneally was fortunate to be captured at sea in the early stages of the war. From 1943, Japan, in contravention of agreements entered into pre-war, adopted a policy of killing all Allied merchant seamen after their vessel was sunk. Japan recognised that Allied, and especially American, shipbuilding capacity was so great that they could never hope to destroy Allied shipping at a faster rate than it could be replaced. So, if the crew of a sinking ship managed to take to the lifeboats they would be killed (the only exception to this was to be men taken for intelligence gathering purposes).

This explains why Captain Walter Hill, from Dublin,[52] stood on the bridge of Japanese submarine I-37 on 22 February 1944 watching his ship's crew being machine gunned in their lifeboats. Hill was the Captain of SS *British Chivalry*, a British merchant vessel on passage from Australia to Abadan. It seems likely that they had been lured into the submarine's operating area with a fake distress signal from a supposedly sinking ship. Regardless, at 10.30 a.m. a torpedo slammed into the *British Chivalry's* engine room. With the engines destroyed, and the ship unable to move, it was only a question of time before they were hit by another torpedo. So the crew took to the boats.

The submarine surfaced, opened fire on the defenceless survivors in the lifeboats, and fired another torpedo at the *British Chivalry*. As soon as the ship sank, the submarine closed the distance to the lifeboats and continued shooting at the men in the boats and in the water. Hill instructed one of his officers to hand semaphore (signal) the submarine, which then ceased firing. The submarine came alongside one of the boats, identified Hill as the ship's Captain and took him onboard. The Japanese then spent an hour or so sailing around and trying to shoot all the men in the water. Fourteen men were killed and many more were wounded, five of whom later died from their wounds.

Amazingly, after the submarine left there were still thirty-eight men alive in the water or lying in the bottom of the damaged boats. After thirty-seven days adrift in an open boat, they were picked up by another British merchant ship. Whether Lieutenant Nakagawa, commanding the submarine, had thought they were all dead or just assumed they would die from wounds will never be known.

Hill, a fervent Irish Republican who hated the British despite commanding a British ship, was interrogated onboard the submarine. Supposedly, he was carrying a briefcase containing valuable jewels when he boarded the submarine. If so, he would not have retained them much longer; though whether or not the jewels were instrumental in his surviving interrogation and being kept onboard is not clear. But what is certain is that Hill was eventually landed in Penang, imprisoned as a military captive, and subjected to the same miseries as the military POWs.

After the war, Lieutenant Nakagawa was indicted for war crimes. In addition to the murder of the *British Chivalry*'s survivors, Nakagawa killed over 100 survivors of the sunken ships *Sutlej* and *Ascot*. He also sank a marked and floodlit hospital ship, with the loss of 296 men and women, whose location had been notified to the Japanese government. Captain Hill refused to give evidence against Nakagawa, though it probably didn't matter too much as Nakagawa disappeared and avoided trial anyway.

7

'THIS IS GALLANTRY, IS IT NOT?'

Around 380 Irishmen were captured when Singapore surrendered on 15 February 1942. Many had been fighting since the Japanese landed in Malaya. Others came late to battle with the arrival of reinforcements in the last weeks of the campaign.

Battery Quartermaster Sergeant (BQMS) Kenneth Cluff, from Stradbally, was captured on Friday 13 February when elements of his gun battery were separated during a withdrawal. He was tied up overnight; the following day, 'along with two others I rejoined my unit [135 Field Regiment] on the 14 February.'[53]

BQMS Cluff was sent back with a message saying that unless Singapore surrendered within twenty-four hours, Singapore would be destroyed, and the other prisoners (captured with him) would be bayoneted. The message was passed along the chain of command and Cluff rejoined his battery. Whether this episode was a serious attempt by the Japanese authorities to bring about a negotiated surrender, or a local initiative by an individual Japanese unit commander is unclear. Cluff: 'The remainder [of the captured men] were shot or bayoneted by the Japs.'[54]

Survival whilst knowing that one's comrades have been murdered is a bitter pill to swallow for any soldier. Cluff was to see even worse in the years to come, and eventually witness the detonation of the atom bombs that bought the war in the Far East to a conclusion. Yet Kenneth Cluff's experience is no worse than many men's, though most cases went unrecorded. In the chaos of the final desperate battle to stop the Japanese advance on Singapore, there were higher priorities than keeping records of individual soldier's actions. And even where documentation was maintained, it was often lost or destroyed during the Japanese occupation. As a result, accounting for the fate of individuals is, to say the least, difficult. But the fate of one unit, the 18th battalion of the Reconnaissance Regiment, typifies soldiers' experiences during the fall of Singapore. The battalion arrived in Singapore during the last few days of the final Japanese assault on the island. There were at least eight Irishmen in the Reconnaissance Regiment.[55] One would be murdered by Japanese soldiers whilst under the protection of the Red Cross. Two more were to die from starvation, disease, and denial of medical treatment. The remaining five survived captivity.

The battalion left India and sailed for Singapore on 23 January 1942 on the *Empress of Asia*, which was carrying over 2,200 soldiers from various units. A little under three weeks later, the *Empress of Asia*, in convoy with some other vessels, arrived at the Banka Straights approaching Singapore. HMS *Exeter*, the cruiser made famous at the battle of the River Plate (against the German cruiser *Admiral Graf Spee*), led the convoy in line astern through the straights. A formation of eighteen Japanese aeroplanes flew overhead at high altitude. One of them dropped a stick of bombs, which landed perilously close to the *Empress*. Columns of water erupted into the air, and shell splinters flew across the decks. No one was injured, however, and the convoy sailed onwards.

Later that morning, the faster ships left the convoy. The three remaining ships, including the *Empress*, headed toward Singapore accompanied by HMS *Danae*. They steamed through the night and arrived at the Sultan Shoal, on the approaches to Singapore, on 5 February 1942. It was a sunny day, with good visibility: ideal weather for the Japanese bombers that attacked the convoy in waves at 11 a.m.

Coming in from all directions, the Japanese bombers dived down to around 3,000 feet and released their bombs. In return, the troopships and the naval escorts opened fire on the aircraft. The scene was a maelstrom of exploding bombs, erupting waterspouts, and the noise of anti-aircraft guns. A bomb hit the *Empress* on the starboard side near the funnel; about ten minutes later, two or three more bombs hit the ship.

Most of the troops were sheltering below deck. About twenty minutes after the attack started, it became clear that the ship would have to be abandoned. Captain Smith, commanding the *Empress of Asia*, instructed the troops to go to their muster stations on A Deck. By now the exploding bombs had started fires down below, and the engine room was abandoned.

At 12 a.m. the Japanese planes broke off the attack. The *Empress* was about 10 or 11 miles off Singapore, and Captain Smith ordered the forecastle crew to drop the anchors. Thick black smoke, and the heat and flames from the fires effectively divided the ship in two as the midship burned fiercely. An Australian sloop, HMAS *Yarra*, came alongside the *Empress'* stern. Many of the soldiers mustered there were able to step directly across and the *Yarra* rescued around 1,000 men.

The situation on the *Empress'* forecastle was more precarious. The troops climbed down ropes into the sea, where small boats waited to pick up the survivors. Many men were transferred by boat, temporarily, to the nearby Sultan Shoal Lighthouse, and some men managed to swim there. Trooper Moran (from Mullingar) struggled in the water, until finally being picked up by a boat. A few men drowned and sharks killed at least one soldier. But, eventually, the troops were landed at Singapore Docks and taken to billets at Geyland Road.

A convoy of trucks took the wounded men to the 1st Malayan General Hospital, a military field hospital set up at Selarang Barracks. The 18th Reconnaissance Battalion set up their HQ at Choon Guan School. The battalion's weapons and equipment were onboard the *Empress of Asia*, which was sinking, and surplus equipment was in short supply. So initially, the men were just given groundsheets, blankets, and mosquito nets. The following day, they were issued with some rifles and Bren guns.

Whilst the battalion was being re-equipped, Patrick Moran, who was feeling ill, reported to the battalion medical officer and was sent to the hospital at Selarang. According to a witness statement from Lieutenant Hargreaves, a Reconnaissance Battalion officer, this was on either 6 or 7 February.

On 11 February, four days before Singapore surrendered to the Japanese, the patients from the field hospital at Selarang Barracks were evacuated to Alexandra Hospital. The hospital had been built in 1940, in the colonial style with long, shaded verandahs and tranquil, well-tended lawns and gardens – though it didn't look quite like this by the time the patients from Selarang arrived there.

Moran was taken to the hospital reception before being allocated to a ward. Corporal Pease, one of the wounded from the *Empress of Asia*, described the sight that met new arrivals at reception:

> … what chaos, wounded men, blood, piles of discarded clothing and equipment, all stained with blood and soil, and the smell was terrible. And as fast as [each] ambulance drove up and discharged its load, another was waiting to do the same thing. Nobody can imagine unless they have seen it what a ghastly, horrible, filthy thing it is … men with legs torn off, heads split, [and] intestines ripped out. I cannot put into words, the sights and sounds, the screams of agony.[56]

During the next couple of days, the hospital suffered constant bombardments and air raids as the Japanese Army advanced closer and closer. By Saturday, 14 February, the hospital was positioned in a small enclave between the British and Japanese front lines. During the afternoon, Japanese infantrymen entered the undefended military hospital. The Japanese soldiers ran amok. They shot doctors and medical staff, raped some auxiliary nurses, and bayoneted to death hundreds of unarmed sick and wounded soldiers.

When a British Army doctor tried to surrender the hospital in order to protect the patients, a Japanese soldier bayoneted him to death through the white flag he was holding. In the hospital reception area, a Japanese soldier walked around beating wounded Allied soldiers with a broom handle as they lay in their beds. Whilst he was doing this, another soldier urinated on a dying man who was lying on the floor. The Japanese even bayoneted an anaesthetised patient on an operating table.

Corporal Patrick Crosbie, from Ballymahon, was an RAMC medical orderly at the hospital. Crosbie: 'Captain Smiley, RAMC, and his staff, carried on with the surgical operation … while the Japs came through … staff and patient were killed and Captain Smiley was left for dead with two bayonet wounds. He carried on work a few hours later.'[57]

In another part of the building, Doctor Allardyce, a former student from Trinity College, Dublin, was being held under guard with some other medical staff. Just before nightfall, the Japanese asked for a doctor. Then they took him away, along with two Royal Army Medical Corps stretcher-bearers. The following day Allardyce was found outside, bayoneted to death. One of the stretcher-bearers was also bayoneted, and the other was found dead with shrapnel wounds.

More Japanese soldiers went into the medical wards where Trooper Moran was located. They bayoneted many of the staff and patients. The ones who were capable of walking were taken into the main corridor. Then they were dragged outside, where around 200 British, Indian, Australian, and Malayan patients and staff were gathered together. These men, many of whom were already badly wounded, were beaten and then tied up. Those who couldn't manage to stand were killed. The survivors, including Moran, unless he had already been murdered, were taken to some buildings on the other side of the Ayer Rajah Road.

At least 200 prisoners were crammed into three rooms. Each unventilated room measured approximately 10 feet by 10 feet.

The men were crushed so closely together that they were forced to urinate over each other. During the night, a number of prisoners died of heat stroke and dehydration.

The next day, 15 February, the prisoners were told they were being taken for a drink of water and led from the rooms in pairs. At first, the men left inside the building believed the Japanese soldiers. But, 'screams of anguish were heard, together with cries in English of "Oh my God", "Mother", "don't, don't", and groans. Then they saw one of the returning Japanese, wiping blood off his bayonet with a large piece of cloth.'[58]

At least 100 men were bayoneted to death before the Japanese were interrupted by artillery fire, which forced them to take cover. One shell blew a hole in the rear of the building and some of the men inside made a run for it. Most of them were machine-gunned by nearby Japanese infantry. But a few prisoners did escape, some of whom survived to bear witness to the massacre.

Patrick Moran was not one of those survivors. He'd been admitted to the hospital a week earlier with what a witness remembered as pneumonia. This was before the advent of antibiotics, and respiratory infections were more often fatal. So it is possible that he, coincidentally, died of pneumonia on 15 February. However, it's more likely that Trooper Moran died, in agony, on the end of a Japanese bayonet.[59]

The seven other Irishmen from the 18th Reconnaissance Battalion had all landed safely from the sinking *Empress of Asia*. They later took part in the most effective counter-attack on Singapore island, as part of a composite force (Tomforce), fighting for the strategic high ground at Bukit Timah. According to Sergeant Cunliffe (18th Reconnaissance Battalion), who later escaped from Singapore:

We moved up north to a rubber plantation where we built a [temporary] camp. Major Spencer called the Company together, showed us a map of the place and explained where the Japanese were. It appeared that they held about one-third of the island [of Singapore] by then.[60]

Tomforce was ordered to capture Bukit Timah village, and the nearby hill. Cunliffe: 'We de-bused in an old ironworks, having been attacked on the way, with no casualties, and put in our attack from there.'[61]

A Japanese officer, Colonel Tsuji, watched the attack go in from the top of Bukit Timah Hill:

> A large force of enemy [British] soldiers surged up the heights like a tidal wave under cover of a barrage. They were supported by armoured cars. It appeared as if the British were staking everything on a counterattack. 'This is gallantry, is it not?' I said to myself, and involuntarily I was lost in admiration.[62]

Gallant indeed, but the attack eventually failed and Tomforce withdrew. Sergeant Cunliffe recalled the aftermath of the attack:

> Some time after that we received orders to withdraw southwards ... to withdraw into Singapore itself to be re-organised. On the Wednesday ... we formed a unit consisting of ourselves [Reconnaissance Regiment], Australian and Indian troops and that morning went up to Bucateema. In the afternoon we were again pushed back into Singapore and as far as I can tell we suffered about 100 casualties. There was constant enemy air activity and ... from Thursday onwards, fighting was confused and small parties of us were endeavouring to mop up enemy infiltration.[63]

The surviving Reconnaissance Regiment soldiers were dispersed throughout Singapore, when the garrison surrendered on 15 February. Some escaped in small boats to Java, and a few eventually made it back home. But the majority went in to captivity. Of the eight Irishmen, one, Patrick Moran, died minutes after becoming a POW. Francis Cullen, from Longford, was captured somewhere on the Bukit Timah Road after the failed counter-attack. A year and a half later he was sent to Thailand to work on the Burma Railway. Totally unfit for travel, never mind hard labour, he died of dysentery inside a cattle truck full of POWs travelling north through Malaya.

William Roe, from Dun Laoghaire, died just over a year later whilst working on the Burma Railway. Christopher Dodgson, from County Tipperary, was captured on Changi Road and later sent to work on the Burma Railway. He survived, as did James Monks, from Dublin, and William Miller, from County Westmeath. Patrick Frain, from Knocknacunny, also lived to return home. So did John Hennessy, from Dublin, after spending much of his captivity underground digging ore out by hand in the copper mines at Kinkaseki, in Formosa.

8

CHANGI

Around 100,000 servicemen marched into captivity when Singapore capitulated. Corporal Wilfred Theakston, from Cork, commented how, on entering into captivity, 'I was searched and my watch and ring taken from me.'[64] Even though theft of valuables was commonplace, it was not consistent. Some Japanese soldiers tore the crucifixes from wounded soldier's necks as they lay in hospital, whilst others allowed POWs to take all they could carry with them into Changi.

In addition to the military personnel, there were hundreds of European women and children in Singapore. Many of them were the families of British and Commonwealth servicemen. The Japanese Army rounded up the women, children, and babies and took them to the civilian jail at Changi. Lieutenant Arthur Cramsie, from Dublin, was one of many soldiers moved by their plight; 'I thanked the almighty that my wife and Patricia, my daughter, were not with them [at Changi Jail]. The women with children had a terrible and unforgiveable experience during the next three and a half years, the mothers half starved themselves trying to keep their children alive.'[65]

Around 50,000 British and Australian soldiers went into Changi Barracks and the married quarters' area. Barbed wire was strung around the exterior and Sikhs, deserters from the Indian Army, patrolled as armed guards working for the Japanese. But initially, aside from making the soldiers line the streets for a humiliating Japanese victory parade, as General Yamashita was filmed driving through Singapore, the Japanese left the POWs to their own devices.

The POWs first priority was repairing bomb damage, restoring the water supplies, and finding ways to accommodate 50,000 men in an area built to house one tenth of that number. The Japanese left the maintenance of discipline inside the camp to the British and Australian officers. The re-imposition of military discipline was not always popular amongst men who felt let down, even sold out. But discipline was the glue that prevented men from turning into an anarchic mob, that otherwise would have descended into chaos and in-fighting.

In the initial period of captivity it was relatively easy to slip away unnoticed; the real prison was created with isolation, not barbed wire. Once clear of Changi, escaped prisoners would need transport to leave the island and then cover the vast distances to the nearest real safety in Ceylon or Australia. Captain Brian Mayne, a doctor from Dublin, recalled, 'A patient of mine, Private Saunderson, in Selarang Hospital … told me he was a fluent Chinese speaker and had [previously] been at large [in 1942] for about one year after the fall of Singapore.'[66]

This is feasible given that the local Chinese population loathed the Japanese and often did all they could to help POWs. Though whether Saunderson was later re-captured or gave himself up isn't clear.

Major Gillachrist Campbell, from Clondalkin, was captured serving with 155 Field Regiment RA and imprisoned in Changi. He was a resourceful and determined man, well aware of the military truism that the sooner an escape attempt is made the more likely it is to succeed. On 19 February, he slipped out of camp at night accompanied by Lieutenant Martin, another artillery officer, and an enlisted soldier, Sapper Morris. They hid up in some mangrove swamps, where it's likely that they had already hid the twelve-foot dinghy that they were to escape in.

The three men left Singapore under cover of darkness. They sailed the dinghy around the harbour boom in what must have been a nerve-wracking adventure, as they slipped past Japanese troops patrolling the harbour in motor launches. Their intention was to skirt Sumatra and sail towards Java and then, if the winds were favourable, try to reach India.

Sailing from Singapore to Java in a tiny dinghy would have been difficult under any circumstances. But doing so without food or water, whilst dodging Japanese air and naval patrols, was an impressive achievement. It took fifteen days to reach Java. At times they tried to land along the coast. But it was difficult to get inshore because of the dense mangrove swamps. Campbell: 'Fifteen days in a small boat is not a joyride! Local storms were unpleasant. But put into some fishermen's huts when exhausted. They fed us and allowed us to sleep despite the fear of Jap patrols.'[67]

Their luck ran out at Merak, in the Sunda Strait, when they sailed into a major Japanese naval force landing troops onto a beachhead. Campbell: '[We were] picked up by a Japanese destroyer after dusk on 6 March ... the Japanese Navy treated us well, in marked contrast to the Army: Transferred to a prison ship, with survivors of [the] cruisers [USS] *Perth* and *Houston*.'[68]

Men captured by the Japanese Navy often reported that their treatment was better than that dished out by the Army. Possibly this was because of the generally higher calibre of recruits to the Japanese Navy. Another possible reason, according to many former POWs, is that the modern Japanese Navy had been founded on the skills and traditions of the (British) Royal Navy and sometimes this showed in the more humane treatment of prisoners.

It's also probable that the three soldiers claimed that they left Singapore prior to the capitulation. This would have been a credible story. It was far too early for there to be any paper trail to contradict them. If so, they would not have been perceived as escaping POWs. Regardless, the men were taken to Batavia and handed over to the Japanese Army.

The fate of other re-captured escapees was far worse. Three men from the Royal Artillery escaped into Singapore, and four Australian soldiers made it as far as Johore. Major William Magill, from Kerry, was carrying his kit in an old wheelbarrow whilst moving to another part of the camp, 'I passed the G.O.C.[69] who was on his return from an unpleasant job attending the shooting of four ORs [other ranks] alleged to have tried to escape.'[70]

According to Magill, who later recorded it in his diary, the GOC recounted the details of the execution to him. The firing party were Sikhs. Their incompetence resulted in a botched execution; numerous rounds were fired into the soldiers' writhing bodies until they finally succumbed to death. Magill:

> A corporal behaved splendidly. He pleaded for one [other] lad, who was very young, that he had ordered this young fellow to accompany him. Then as usual the firing party made a mess of it. All [the POWs] were splendid. The corporal was first shot in the arm, then in the leg, after which he told the firing party to carry on 'shoot me in the heart and finish the job'.[71]

It's every soldier's duty to attempt to escape from captivity. Though, the reality is that few attempt it and even fewer are successful. After the execution of the first escapees, the Japanese took further measures to deter break outs. Sergeant Dermot MacDonough, from County Kildare, 2nd battalion East Surrey Regiment: 'We were forced to sign papers undertaking not to attempt escape, and were given to understand that should one escape ten of his comrades would be executed.'[72]

The Japanese forced them to sign by moving all the British and Australian POWs into Selarang Barracks on 30 August. Around 17,000 men were crammed into a space designed for 800. They dug latrines in the grassed area in front of the buildings and did their best to maintain hygiene and provide food. After a few days men started dying from dysentery. Then the Japanese threatened to bring all the sick and wounded men from the hospitals into the compound too. It was obvious that with the addition of hundreds of wounded men the already dire conditions would worsen and an epidemic of diseases would decimate the troops.

Eventually the senior British and Australian officers instructed the POWs to sign the *pro forma* 'promising not to escape'. As a promise made under extreme duress it was meaningless, either morally or legally. But the Japanese had set a precedent at Selarang, that any resistance to their commands would be met with extreme, even lethal, violence.

The Japanese used the POWs as forced labourers, clearing roads and repairing damage from the fighting. The men were generally taken out in working parties under the nominal command of a British officer, with Japanese guards directing work. Whilst the conditions were nowhere near as bad as things would later get on the Burma Railway, the work was usually manual, backbreaking, and spurred on with beatings.

Lieutenant Clancy (Dublin), now recovered from his wounds, commanded a working party sometime in the latter part of 1942. They were employed building a shrine for the Japanese. The men were allowed a ten-minute break in the afternoon to drink some unsweetened black tea. Clancy noticed that two of the soldiers hadn't had a chance to get a drink, a vital necessity in the tropical heat. Later in the day he called the two men out of the chain gang and took them into a jungle clearing to brew up some tea. The Japanese guards observing this ran over and, despite Clancy's protestations, made the two men stand to attention for hours on top of a mound of earth, sweating and dehydrated. One of the two soldiers was Sidney Lockwood, who later commented on the injustice and stupidity of the Japanese soldier's actions in response to Lieutenant Clancy's simple kindness in trying to get a cup of tea for his men.

Once back within Changi the POWs were still left mostly to their own devices. Various lectures and classes were put on to obviate the boredom that characterises POW life. At this stage many of the POWs were still physically healthy enough to participate. Military discipline also continued to be enforced at Changi. This was in everyone's long-term interest. But there were some, including officers and long-term career soldiers, who felt that at Changi it sometimes went too far.

Major Earnest Fillmore, from Dublin, was an experienced soldier who had been in the British Army since 1904. He was hardly likely to be over-sensitive to military discipline. But after the war he formally reported what he considered to be excessive, perhaps even unlawful, levels of punishment. Fillmore:

> The punishments inflicted on POW other ranks by Lieutenant Colonel Newey [Straits Settlements Volunteer Force] whilst acting as administrative officer, Changi Gaol … were in excess of the powers laid down … for a commanding officer … numerous NCOs and men who I came into contact with were very bitter as it was bad enough to be semi-starved and made to work for the Japanese.[73]

All armies use punishments in response to breaches of military regulations. In normal circumstances these punishments are codified, clear cut, and authorised by the respective government. But Allied officers commanding troops in Japanese custody had to maintain internal discipline, whilst lacking the sanctions normally available to them. So, whilst stealing from the Japanese was not considered wrong, stealing from, say, the POW cookhouse was a serious crime because food was in such short supply that any loss meant another already starving man would then go without. In cases like this, or disobeying an order, etc., Allied officers and NCOs had two choices – they could either pass the matter on to the Japanese, which was unthinkable, or improvise a punishment. The options were some form of confinement, in a hut, or being beaten up by a couple of senior NCOs. The most serious option was to have a man's rations reduced.

Not surprisingly, the imposition of discipline and punishments was resented by some. But in camps where there was a lack of effective control by the senior officers and NCOs rackets, theft, and bullying, from a few unscrupulous men, could cause chaos. However, it wasn't only the enlisted men who felt aggrieved at what was sometimes considered excessive and officious impositions of disciplinary codes. J. A. Richardson, an officer in the First Independent Company, Malayan Volunteers, complained bitterly about what he saw as pointless and petty discipline. Richardson:

> Of course ... if the Japs were not bothering us, someone or other of the British officer hierarchy would dream up schemes to disrupt our lifestyle. [I was transferred to another officer's mess] presided over by a Major Tottenham [from Mullingar]. Tottenham was a petty tyrant to whom I took an instant dislike.[74]

Richardson injured his leg and was medically excused from camp chores, which included gardening – growing food. Richardson: 'Tottenham claimed that I was swinging the lead and ordered me out to work ... this order, presumably motivated by spite, was rescinded on the advice of the doctor and I was allowed to rest the damaged leg.'[75]

Clashes of personality were not uncommon, and theft and rackets, in some POW camps, were never entirely eradicated. Men in captivity are subject to mental and physical stress, challenging the abilities of those in authority to manage difficult situations and the capacity of those under command to accept discipline. The reality is that problems were inevitable.

Whilst discipline was sometimes a source of strife at Changi, religion was a far less contentious matter. The Japanese did nothing to prevent religious worship there, though this was not the norm in other camps. One British soldier recalled:

> Strangely enough, there was little enough interference by the Japanese in religious matters [at Changi]. One incident brought home to me that there must be a sprinkling

of Christians in the ranks of our captors. Irishman Paddy
Kennedy[76] and I were marching to a work assignment
(shirtless) with a diminutive Jap guard shuffling alongside.
Paddy had a chain around his neck from which hung a cru-
cifix which caught the Jap's eye. Pointing to Paddy he asked,
'You Ca-to-lic?' On receiving Paddy's reply in the affirma-
tive, he followed up with, 'You prees hab wifo?' (Your priest
have wife?) 'No,' replied Paddy with a shake of his head. 'Ah
so,' responded the Jap, 'Me Ca-to-lic too.[77]

It's reasonable to assume that a majority of Southern Irish
POWs were Roman Catholics. There were at least four
Catholic priests: Father Richard Kennedy and Father Kevin
Whelan from Dublin; Father James Ward, from Galway; and
Father John O'Mahoney. O'Mahoney told the Japanese that
he originally came from Queen's County, instead of using
the name Laois as it was called after the establishment of the
Irish Free State in 1922. Whether this was a reflection of his
political beliefs and allegiances is not clear. Regardless, they
were all commissioned officers in the Royal Army Chaplains'
Department ministering to the spiritual needs of Catholics
serving in the British Army.

Father Kennedy worked on the Railway at Konyu and
Hintok Mountain. He ensured that Roman Catholics had
their own chapel area separate from the Church of England.
Though, chapels on the Railway tended to be little more than
a designated area in camp, at best, and not a chapel in the sense
of a building.

Priests, of any faith, are not mentioned in POW memoirs in
the same way that doctors and medical staff are. Nor do they
figure prominently in official documentation. Immediately
after the war, Irish POWs were asked to point out any acts of
courage and distinguished service carried out by other POWs
whilst in captivity. In response, many of them lauded the medical services. But there is little mention of the clergy, with the

notable exception of (Church of England) Padre Duckworth, who was deeply respected; though this was possibly as much for his courage in standing up to the Japanese as it was for any religious reason.

Being a member of the clergy of any faith was viewed with suspicion by the Japanese. Holy Orders gave no defence from Japanese atrocities as the following incident, which was just one of many, shows. Japanese soldiers bayoneted to death two Roman Catholic priests and two nuns in the village of Tasimboko. The bodies of the two nuns, both young women, were naked when they were found. An older nun, aged around sixty, had been allowed to escape.[78]

The horrors of Japanese captivity challenged the religious convictions of many. A former POW recalled, in conversation with this author, that soon after he was imprisoned by the Japanese he fell into conversation with a Padre. He recalled that the Padre exhorted him to look to God for help and inspiration, whilst in captivity. A few months later the POW met the same Padre again and the subject of God came up – in response, the Padre said something along the lines of, 'oh, don't bother with all that old nonsense.'[79]

Being a priest in the British armed services was never easy at the best of times. To the soldier the priest was the 'Bible basher'; to the sailor he was the 'sin bosun'. Before the war, soldiers in barracks attended compulsory church parade each Sunday: a best-uniform spit-and-polish duty resented by many. But in the prison camps church services, when allowed, were often moving and inspirational occasions, regardless of a man's faith or lack of it. Soldiers singing well-known hymns together in some jungle clearing, or sick men quietly chanting the familiar words of the Lord's Prayer in the darkness of a bamboo death hut, provided strength to some and comfort to others.

Marine John Wisecup, an American serviceman from the USS *Houston*, worked on the Burma Railway. He was one of a group of servicemen given the task of burying cholera victims at Hintok. Initially they dug individual graves. But the death toll became so great that they were unable to keep up with it. Wisecup remembered working with an Irishman, from Dublin, who he called Paddy. Paddy was very religious. Wisecup suggested that they dig one big hole and put all the bodies in together. Paddy objected to this on the grounds that it was sacrilegious. But pragmatism won out and they agreed to use a common grave.

Both men were themselves sick with the usual gamut of tropical diseases. They were lice ridden, starving, half naked and barefoot. They staggered along a jungle path carrying a corpse between them. The dead man's feet kept knocking into Wisecup and, losing his temper, he threw the corpse into the jungle. This was too much for Paddy who made his feelings plain when he told Wisecup that no good would come of blaspheming the dead.[80]

We do not know with certainty if Paddy was a Catholic. There is evidence though that a strong Catholic faith helped some of the Irish POWs to survive the camps. Captain Michael Murphy (Cork) was imprisoned at Mitsushima Camp (Japan) for the last four months of the war. It was one of Japan's most brutal camps, with vicious guards; nine of whom were executed for war crimes after the war. Murphy was there during that dreadful hiatus between the dropping of the first and second atomic bombs, and like all the other POWs, he had good reason to meditate deeply on just what would happen next.

The POWs knew that the end of their existence was a very real, and imminent, possibility. Practically, there was little that they could do. Some waited, fearful and concerned. Others were resigned to whatever fate brought, seeing death as no worse than their present misery. Murphy, like many others, turned to God. His deep Catholic faith was made plain by the Novena he made, to Our Lady for the Assumption, appealing for peace and protection in the final stages of the attack.

9

EXODUS

Many civilians and non-essential service personnel were evacuated from Singapore in the early stages of the campaign in Malaya. But there was reluctance, by both the authorities and many individuals, to be seen to be deserting the sinking ship. So opportunities to move civilians out of Singapore, when an orderly planned evacuation was feasible, were missed.

Maurice O'Connell, from Dublin, was one of the civilians who did escape successfully, well before the Japanese Army reached Singapore. His father, Basil O'Connell, served as Commandant of the Police Training Depot in Singapore. He was determined not to see his family fall into Japanese hands, and arranged their evacuation. Maurice O'Connell:

> I remember very little, being only five years old. My father put my mother, my three week old brother and I, on a boat just as quickly as he could. My father, as a 'local expert' with the remnants of his [police] trainees formed a kind of informal task force working with the Army. After the capitulation he ended up being interned in the old criminal jail building as a civilian internee. It was tough but they didn't have the same sort of deliberate extreme humiliation meted out to the soldiers. [But] my father didn't have an easy time. I have a photo taken of him a week or so after liberation and it's one of those classic walking skeleton pictures. I've no doubt that it contributed to his early death.[81]

Hundreds of small ships left Singapore in a tragic exodus during the last few days before (and sometimes just after) the capitulation. They were instructed to head south to Batavia. Unknown to the authorities, this put them on a collision course with a Japanese invasion force heading towards Java. Many ships fell prey to relentless air attacks before this, as the Japanese air force now had complete mastery of the air. Ironically, in some cases, this was their salvation as survivors were picked up by small boats and fed into a secret supply route set up by Colonel Warren.

The supply route started in the west Sumatran port of Padang, then followed roads and railways to the Indragiri river, and across to the east coast. Then the route followed the Lingga and Riouw Islands up to Singapore. This route was successfully followed (in reverse) by many survivors of the small ships sunk *en route* to Java. Though others, such as Wing Commander George Atkins, were less fortunate.

Wing Commander Atkins RAF, from County Cork, served on the staff of RAF HQ Far East Command in Singapore. During the last few days before Singapore fell to the Japanese, Atkins commanded a small HQ staff of signals and cypher (code) personnel. They operated from various locations, moving on to set up elsewhere each time their offices were destroyed by Japanese bombing.

The last few surviving RAF Hurricane fighters had been withdrawn from Singapore to Java and the ground crews were being evacuated in whatever small ships and boats that could be found. The Army no longer needed Atkins' signals staff in Singapore. So, on the morning of 13 February, Air Vice-Marshall Pulford, the Air Officer Commanding (AOC), gave Atkins permission to evacuate his men onboard Motor Launch 310 (ML310). Atkins:

> I then went back to my temporary HQ with one officer, Pilot Officer Walker, who had volunteered to remain with

me. We cleaned up and destroyed everything and I then went to Fort Canning where I found two pilots who were 'walking wounded' from the hospital. I saw General Percival and collected his A.D.C. and a small party including [around ten] 'walking wounded' and took them to the wharf.[82]

They drove through streets blocked with rubble from burning godowns (warehouses) and entered the docks at Clifford Pier. A naval officer directed some of the airmen and the wounded men to one of the evacuation ships. Atkins, with the remainder of the group, walked along to the end of the wharf where ML310 was tied up at the jetty.

Air Vice-Marshall Pulford, and Rear Admiral Spooner, by now the senior naval officer left in Singapore, were already onboard ML310. Accounts differ as to exactly when they departed from Singapore. But according to Atkins they sailed the following morning carrying forty-seven personnel, from all three services, with Lieutenant J. Bull RNVR in command of ML310.

The ML slowly sailed out of the harbour with the Admiral and the Air Marshal stood on the bridge, watching the pall of smoke hanging over the burning city. One of the ML's officers, Lieutenant Pool, later described Wing Commander Atkins as looking quiet and reflective. And Atkins had much to reflect on, as he stood alongside a naval officer, Commander Frampton, silently contemplating the scene of defeat and disaster that lay behind them.

Soon after leaving harbour, the launch developed problems with the steering gear and ran onto a reef. The crew threw as much heavy equipment as possible overboard, in order to make the launch lighter, so that it floated off. But in the process of lightening ship and repairing the steering gear, one of the officers, Lieutenant Pool, was injured. He crushed two fingers when his hand was caught between a dinghy and the side of the launch. This was to lead to a change of plan that would later have disastrous repercussions.

ML310 sailed to a small island south-west of Monkey Island. The crew took the boat in near to the shore and put up camouflage nets to hide it from patrolling Japanese aircraft. As soon as it became dark, they sailed onwards to the Seven Brothers Islands (about 25 miles from Banka) and again laid-up and remained hidden.

The original plan had been to sail under the cover of darkness, keeping the launch camouflaged up in the many small islands during daylight. By now the Japanese had total air superiority and were able to bomb and destroy anything they sighted. Admiral Spooner was worried about Lieutenant Pool's medical condition. Pool's whole left arm was swollen and inflamed and he was suffering from a fever. So Spooner decided that they should continue in daylight and try to get to Muntok to find a doctor. It was a compassionate decision, though perhaps not the wisest choice in terms of the overall safety of the group.

They sailed around midday and headed towards the Banka Straits, which they needed to pass through in order to escape. Atkins: 'On approaching Banka Island we sighted five destroyers in line ahead and two cruisers. We turned tail and ran for it, but their aircraft attacked and the ships opened fire.'[83]

They opened fire with the twin Lewis guns at one of the Japanese seaplanes attacking the launch, and the planes flew off. But trying to fight powerful Japanese warships from a small motor launch, armed with a tiny three-pounder gun, would have been suicidal and pointless. Escape was the only sane option. And they headed towards the nearest island, possibly Pulau Perkajang. Then they ran onto one of the reefs that abound in that area.

Admiral Spooner ordered all the passengers to wade ashore and take cover in the jungle, hoping that the Japanese would not realise that the launch had been carrying anyone but the crew. Atkins:

I decided to remain with the ship. A destroyer which was now detached from the main force, opened fire and we [the officers] decided to give the remaining crew a chance for their lives and ordered them to swim ashore. The Japs then sent a boarding party and, after searching and lining us up on the after deck with our hands up and other unpleasantness, started to smash the engines and gear in the ship.[84]

The boarding party was under the command of a Japanese Midshipman who had been ordered to make the ML unusable. Atkins' comment about the 'other unpleasantness' is a polite euphemism for the beating that the Japanese routinely gave to prisoners. Atkins had already dumped all the secret documents overboard that had been carried with the Admiral's staff. And he told the Midshipman that there were only thirteen crewmen, and that these were the men that had been seen swimming ashore.

After searching the ML, and wrecking the engine, the Japanese lined the British officers up against the guardrails at the stern. According to Lieutenant Pool, Atkins voiced everyone's thoughts when he muttered a comment that the Japanese were about to shoot them.[85] The Japanese Midshipman stood there for a minute or so. He held his sword whilst the boarding party waited, weapons pointing at the officers, for the command to open fire. Then, for some reason, the Midshipman changed his mind. He pointed the men into the dinghy and they climbed in expecting at any time to be shot in the back.

As they headed towards the island, waiting, tensed, for the shots to come, one of the officers looked back towards the Japanese. The boarding party was heading back in their boat to the destroyer. Much relieved, the men rowed ashore in the dinghy and met up with the remainder of the group. The ML was clearly beyond repair and the only options were either to sit and wait until the Japanese eventually returned or to find some way of sending for help.

The native inhabitants had already left the island, but two Javanese officials, working for the Dutch colonial administration, were still there. They helped to find and repair a small prau (a narrow open sailing boat). Lieutenant Bull, two naval ratings, and the two Javanese were then sent to Java to find help.

The party departed on their 300-mile trip around 19 or 20 February. A week later the prau was sighted by a small flotilla of Australian and Dutch warships anchored at Merak, Java. The men were taken onboard HMAS *Maryborough*. A signal was sent out which was picked up by the US HQ in Java, and an American submarine was sent to the island on a rescue mission. Unfortunately, despite running great risks travelling through seas dominated by the Japanese Navy, the submarine failed to locate the survivors. US Navy submariners landed at night from a rubber dinghy. But they failed to make contact with anyone, and it seems likely that a navigational error took them to the wrong island.

All this was unknown to Wing Commander Atkins and the rest of the party. At first morale was high. But as they waited in vain for rescue, with very little food, men started dying from starvation and disease, especially malaria. Air Vice-Marshall Pulford died in March and Rear Admiral Spooner died in April. The men grew weaker and weaker. Lieutenant Stonor:

> The island was very malarial. Atkins had fever badly and for the last month [on the island] had it practically every night and became too weak to do very much … When we realised that we were not going to be rescued a large number of men seemed to give up hope, which with fever was the cause of many of the deaths. After a while it became an awful effort … even bringing in food. There was no doctor in the party and no one knew anything about tropical diseases except Atkins.[86]

Despite taking quinine, which they were well supplied with, men were dying from cerebral malaria. By late April, eighteen of the original party were dead. It was clear to the rest that unless they found a way to escape from the island that they would all die.

Another old, and damaged, prau was found. The party set to repairing it as best they could, using bits of old canvas and kerosene cans to try to make it watertight. By now they had been on the island for three months and they were all ill and debilitated. Atkins decided to take some of the relatively fitter men, including Able Seaman Ronald Johnson, from Dublin, with him to find help. They intended to set sail for Sumatra and then send a rescue party back to the island for the remainder. They were unsure whether or not Sumatra was now in Japanese hands. But, even had they known, it's hard to see what else they could have done.

After a hazardous seventy-mile voyage in their leaky little boat, they were wrecked on a lee shore on an island, Pulau Saya. Some Malay fishermen took them to Sinkep, in return for a payment of $200. When they landed on Sinkep they discovered that the whole Southern region was now occupied by the Japanese. So, stranded without food, water, or a boat, their situation was hopeless. The only way now to help the men left back on the island was to surrender. Atkins:

> I surrendered and the Japanese collected the rest of the party and the sick from Puloe Perkajang. We were then brought to Singapore by the Japanese, and after interrogation for several days, the O.R.s [other ranks] were brought to P.O.W. Camp, Changi. Lieutenants Pool, Stoner and myself were kept in Jap. Gestapo [Kempeitai] HQ for 15 days.[87]

The Kempeitai were the Japanese Army's Military Police. Despite nominal legal controls, in practice they had absolute power of life and death over soldiers and civilians alike in Japan and the Japanese occupied territories. One of their duties was the interrogation of POWs.

The three officers were questioned in turn, over a period of several days. They were asked to divulge military information, which under international law no POW is obliged to do. Lieutenant Pool was interrogated by a Kempeitai Colonel, who held a sword across the back of his neck and threatened to cut his head off if he didn't cooperate. Atkins had an equally nasty experience: 'I was threatened with torture and various unpleasantness, was given an ocular demonstration of torture performed on an unfortunate Chinese and then [I was] beaten.'[88]

Eventually, the Kempeitai gave up, perhaps realising that three months after having left Singapore Atkins would not have any information worth the effort involved in beating it out of him. Atkins was taken to Changi POW Camp; he spent the following three years in Changi, Selarang, and finally Changi Gaol. In 1946, George Atkins was awarded the OBE, 'in recognition of distinguished services rendered during operations in the Far East'.

10

FLIGHT OF THE ANGELS

During the last few days of fighting in Singapore the defensive perimeter grew smaller and smaller. As the Japanese advanced, the military hospitals were evacuated and patients and staff absorbed into Changi and Alexandra Military Hospitals. The authorities knew of the savage massacre at St Stephen's Hospital, in Hong Kong, when it surrendered to the Japanese. Many of the nurses had been raped. In some instances Japanese soldiers murdered the nurses after raping them and then mutilated their corpses. So despite the desperate need for nurses to tend the growing number of wounded, it was decided to evacuate the Singapore nurses.

The nursing staff started leaving the hospitals on 11 February. Most were reluctant to abandon the wounded soldiers in their care and only left after being ordered to. Over the next two days, parties of nurses boarded ships leaving Singapore. Some eventually reached safety in Ceylon or Australia. But many died in Japanese naval and air attacks on the evacuation ships.

One of the last groups of nurses left the Alexandra Military Hospital on 13 February. They made their way to the docks to embark on a small (954 ton) passenger vessel, the *Kuala*. There were thousands of women, children, male civilians, and servicemen trying to escape from Singapore. At the same time, Japanese aircraft were bombing the docks. It was a scene of chaos and confusion. Understandably, people were more concerned with survival than compiling accurate passenger lists. Where records were kept they were often destroyed when the ships themselves sank. And even immediately after the war, when many witnesses were still alive, it was impossible to compile definitive passenger and survival lists. This account must be read with that in mind.

Somewhere between 600 and 700 passengers and crew sailed on the *Kuala* on 13 February. There were a number of Irish girls amongst the fifty (Queen Alexandra's Imperial Military Nursing Service [QAs]) nurses onboard. These included Mary Cooper, Edith Pedlow, Ruth Dickson, Edith Carroll, Irene Wright, and Charlotte Black.[89] A Japanese bomb landed on the ship whilst it was still in Singapore docks and some nurses were amongst the fatalities. They were buried at sea the following day; Sister Edith Carroll may have been amongst them.

Kuala sailed through the night and then anchored the following morning close to Pom Pong Island,[90] intending to hide during the day whilst the Japanese Air Force was most active. Soon after this, the *Kuala* was bombed by Japanese aircraft. The ship was both on fire and sinking. Those who weren't killed by the bombing jumped into the water. One of the QA nurses, Sister Margot Turner, recalled, 'The sea was covered with dead, dying and swimming people. The Japanese planes came over four times, dive-bombing the *Kuala* and machine-gunning the swimmers.'[91] Sister Irene Wright probably died around this time, either onboard the ship or soon after in the water.

Around 250 women and children got ashore on Pom Pong Island. Turner: 'There were seven Q.A.s with me [including] Sisters Pedlow, Black and Cooper. A naval officer on the beach told us that there were other survivors on the far side of Pom Pong.'[92]

Some of the nurses went around the island to join the other survivors. Sister Turner followed them soon after. Meanwhile, Japanese bombers were finishing off the ships and firing at the women and children on the island with machine guns. After this the nurses got on with the grim task of caring for the wounded. Turner:

There was plenty of work for me and the other Sisters to do as the many wounded and sick needed all our attention. The

Sisters tore strips off their already tattered dresses to make bandages. We were all rationed to one biscuit and half a mug of water a day. Our medical supplies were few and very precious; but at least we had some morphia which made the last hours of the mortally wounded more bearable. Many of them were past recovery. There was no medical officer but the Sisters divided themselves into shifts [to care for the wounded day and night].[93]

Sister Pedlow distinguished herself caring for the wounded. She was honoured with a mention in Despatches, in recognition of her courage and devotion to duty during the sinking of the *Kuala* and her work on Pom Pong Island.

Corporal Terence McGahan, from County Cavan, was one of the uninjured servicemen and civilians who assisted the nurses in caring for the wounded. He was amongst a party of RAF technicians evacuated onboard a Chinese merchant vessel, the *Tien Kwang*, which accompanied the *Kuala* from Singapore and was also destroyed in the Japanese attack.

The following night McGahan was taken by prou (canoe) to a nearby island, where he thought he might get treatment for his malaria from some stranded RAMC personnel. There were also naval officers on the island searching for boats and evacuating small groups. McGahan joined a party of officers and men from his own RAF unit, and tried to sail through the Banka Straits.

McGahan was a Dunkirk veteran. He'd managed to escape by making his way on foot along the beaches, until he found a small fishing boat which took him to Folkestone. But he was not so fortunate this time. On 19 February, he landed on Banka Island, which was already occupied by the Japanese. McGahan:

I was herded into a barbed wire circle ... with men, women, and children. Forty of those who were imprisoned were

Australian nurses. They were all sorted out and taken away out of the compound. That was the last journey 39 of them made. During the night, we lay on the grass of this island and listened to their screams and cries for help as they were raped and ravaged by the Jap troops. It was the worst night of my life.[94]

Back on Pom Pong Island, a small ship, the *Tanjong Penang*, arrived and offered to take off some of the wounded. It was already heavily loaded with around 200 women, children, and soldiers, many rescued from sunken ships and boats. Some of the wounded were carried onboard. Then the captain of the *Tanjong Penang* asked if some nurses would come onboard to help care for them.

It's impossible to know with certainty what happened to Sister Black. It may be that she stayed on the island and was rescued by another boat, which was later sunk by the Japanese air force. Or she may have left on the *Tanjong Penang* and died after landing on Banka Island. But whether from drowning or the effects of her wounds, she died on 24 February.

Sister Cooper and Sister Dickson may have left on the *Tanjong Penang*, or they may have stayed and been taken off the island by another vessel. Both eventually made it to Sumatra as prisoners of the Japanese Army. Sister Dickson died in captivity on Christmas Eve 1944.

Sister Turner and Sister Pedlow *were* amongst the nurses caring for the wounded onboard the *Tanjong Penang*, which left Pom Pong early on 17 February. They worked constantly throughout the day and were exhausted by the time it was dark. They'd just settled down on the upper deck to get some sleep, when the unarmed *Tanjong Penang* was attacked by a Japanese warship near Banka Island. Turner: 'A searchlight blazed down on us and, without warning, there were two violent explosions as two shells hit the ship … there were people dead and dying all around us … a ghastly shambles of mutilated bodies.'[95]

The little ship sank quickly. Sister Turner found herself in the water amongst a helpless mess of drowning children, screaming wounded, and desperate swimmers, all clinging onto whatever wreckage might keep them afloat. Over the next two or three days, those survivors who got on to one of the small rafts had the miserable experience of watching the small children dying from thirst and heatstroke. Others lived long enough to be washed up on Banka Island. But their ordeal wasn't over as many of them were murdered, including some of the nurses.

Sister Pedlow survived for at least two days after the sinking. She may have died on the rafts or been bayoneted to death on the beach by Japanese soldiers. Margot Turner was picked up by a Japanese ship after four days drifting in the Java Sea. Luckily, the ship's (Japanese) doctor had been trained in America and spoke English, and ensured she was treated decently whilst onboard. She was landed in Muntok harbour, on Banka Island and taken to a civilian internment camp where she met up with Mary Cooper.

The inmates of the camp in Muntok were taken to another camp in Palembang. Initially the internees were under the control of the Japanese civil authorities. Conditions weren't too bad, though families were separated with men being put in one camp, and women and children in another. The internees later came under the direct control of the Japanese Army. Then the standard regime of slave labour, starvation, and brutality, became the norm. The Imperial Japanese Army made no concessions for women.

Sister Cooper and Sister Turner were military personnel, and they asked to be put with the military prisoners. Despite this, they were kept with the civilian women at Palembang. Then in October 1942, the Japanese commandant offered them (along with two civilian nurses) the opportunity to work in a nearby hospital assisting a Dutch doctor giving medical care to local civilians. The nurses agreed to this. Initially things went well, and they were sometimes allowed to visit a hospital camp housing sick (Allied) POWs and internees. Cooper and Turner were in the rare position of having passes which allowed them to travel between the local hospital, the market, and the POW hospital. They took advantage of this to smuggle messages and to try to get some extra food back to the internees.

One day they decided to walk to a nearby military POW camp to talk, through the perimeter, to the prisoners. Turner:

> We found the camp alright and the men were delighted to see us; but when we saw a Japanese car approaching we went on walking as if we didn't know the camp was there. The car passed us and then turned round and came back towards us. I said to Mary, 'We had better turn around and walk back towards the hospital'. The car stopped and two Japanese got out and asked us what we were doing. I replied, 'We are hospital nurses – we have been for a walk and now we are going back to the hospital'.[96]

The Japanese officers tried to make the two girls get into the car. They refused and so the officers took their passes away. Turner: 'Eventually … we did get our passes back … but poor Mary Cooper was so terrified that she vowed she would never go out again.'[97]

From March 1943 onwards Cooper and Turner were prevented from visiting the POW hospital again. The general discipline at their hospital worsened with the appointment of a Japanese doctor in command. On 4 April the two girls, plus the Dutch doctor and his wife, were taken to the offices of the Kempeitai (Japanese military police). The doctor and his wife were beaten up and put in prison, whilst Cooper and Turner were sent back to the hospital.

Turner, Cooper, and the two civilian nurses were asked by the Japanese doctor if they wanted to continue working at the hospital or return to the civilian internment camp. The girls said that they wanted to go back to the camp and the Japanese then put them in prison.

The Japanese Army provided what it euphemistically called 'comfort women' for the Japanese soldiers. Tens of thousands of Chinese, Korean, Taiwanese, and some European women, were forced to work in Japanese Army brothels. Cooper and Turner were probably saved from this by the order sent from military headquarters in Japan, to the local command in Java and Sumatra, instructing them to release Dutch (and other European) women from the brothels and not to use Dutch women anymore.

Sister Cooper and Sister Turner were thrown into a bare cell together with only a straw mat on the floor to sleep on. Turner:

> We were allowed out of the cell twice a day for about five minutes. The sanitary arrangements can be left to the imagination. We had two very meagre meals a day and sometimes either cold tea or water. Our fellow prisoners were murderers or thieves, Malayan or Chinese. But they were very good to us so far as they were able, knowing that discovery would mean some sort of brutal punishment. When they went out on working parties they would sometimes pass through the bars to us some black coffee in a tin or maybe a banana or a bit of cake ... our cell was large enough for us to walk four paces and that was our exercise.[98]

Two or three months later, Cooper and Turner were placed in another cell with the two civilian nurses. The Kempeitai had rounded up a lot of new prisoners and space had to be made for them. Turner: 'Terrible things started to happen in the jail; the prisoners were beaten and tortured and many of them died as a result. The things we saw were so horrible that I still can't bear to think, much less talk, about them.'[99]

In September 1943, after six months' imprisonment, all four nurses were released from prison and returned to the civilian internment camp. Their physical condition was appalling; even compared to the skeletal inmates of the camp, most of whom now weighed less than seven stones. Betty Jeffrey, an Australian nurse, kept a secret diary. She recorded her impressions when Cooper and Turner arrived in her camp, though she gives the date as February 1944:[100]

> They looked terrible, and had a definitely wild look in their eyes, which is not to be wondered at. They had been treated very badly by the Japanese … amazingly enough they were quite sane when they joined us again, but one lass had to go into our camp hospital for some weeks.[101]

Of course there was very little that could be done for the girls in the camp hospital, except for tender loving care, as the Japanese denied POWs and internees access to drugs and medicines. Mary Cooper never recovered her health. In April 1945, when the camp was moved to another location she had to be transported on a stretcher. Then her condition worsened due to beri-beri.

The Japanese camp authorities, realising that they might be called upon to account for their crimes after the war, decided that Irish nurses could leave the camp. Of course, no one trusted the Japanese. According to her friend Margot Turner, Mary was 'terrified at having to go'. Betty Jeffrey recorded in her diary on 26 May:

> Mary Cooper … was suddenly called upon about a month ago by two Jap officers and told to hurry up and get well because she could go home to Ireland. Just like that! Mary felt very mixed about the whole thing. She was desperately ill and she wanted to go home, but not alone like that.[102]

Exactly one month later Betty Jeffrey wrote, 'No Ireland for poor little Mary Cooper – she … died this morning. Mary was an awfully nice girl, only in her twenties, too.'[103]

11

GUNNER 600

In October 1942, 600 soldiers from the Royal Artillery were loaded onto a former coal ship in Singapore docks. Conditions onboard were horrendous. They were crammed below in the hold without food, water, ventilation, or any sanitary arrangements, suffering from heat exhaustion, dehydration, and dysentery. And during the voyage Japanese troops amused themselves by pouring buckets of urine through the hatches onto the POWs below.

The men were destined for the Solomon Islands. Eighty-two badly sick men were disembarked *en route* at Rabaul, on 6 November 1942. Only eighteen of them survived the war; including Lance Bombardier Patrick Ahern, from Fermoy, County Cork and Lance Sergeant Patrick (Nobby) Nolan from Wexford.

They were put to work unloading cargo from a Japanese ship. One of the gunners had a wound on his back which broke open. Regardless, he was ordered to continue carrying sacks of rice. When he objected, he was tied to a tree and tortured. The Japanese soldiers tried to make him drink urine – the only fluids they would allow him to have. When he refused they beat him and poured a bucket of urine over his head. Then they stripped him, rubbed animal manure over his genitals, and left him (tied to the tree) to be tormented by hordes of tropical biting insects. The following morning he was taken away and murdered.[104]

Patrick Ahern ripped holes in the rice sacks destined for Japanese troops whilst working in Wide Bay unloading ships. The POWs also tried to steal food. Gunner O'Connor, from Dublin, managed to smuggle a heavy box back into camp. The effort and risk involved was tremendous. So it must have been a grim joke, to a starving man, to finally open the box and find it contained horseshoes.

Another prisoner, BQMS Stokes, contracted diphtheria. The guards ordered him to be isolated to protect themselves from infection. Sergeant Nolan volunteered to stay with Stokes and nurse him. But without medicines or even food and fresh water it was a hopeless task and Stokes died on 28 November. Malaria took a bigger toll and ten POWs died within the first two months. This was an unnecessary tragedy which could have been prevented by using some of the plentiful stocks of quinine.

Food rations, never plentiful, were cut even further. Boiled rice augmented with a little stolen dried fish was insufficient in quality or quantity to maintain life. Within a year sixty-one of the original eighty-two POWs were dead. In growing desperation, the survivors took bigger and bigger risks to get food. The Japanese soldiers had a stock of tinned fish that was too far from camp to get to at night. So some of the POWs decided to chance raiding it at midday when the guards generally rested in the heat. Patrick Aherne, along with two other gunners, Gabbert and Fowler, went out and got three cases of fish and brought them back to camp. As they were throwing the cases over the fence, Ahern noticed some Japanese soldiers coming. The three men ran for it but Gabbert was caught.

The Japanese took Gabbert back to camp and started kicking and beating him. Aherne and Fowler owned up to being the other two men that had been seen, knowing that if they didn't the guards would punish every prisoner. The three men were stood in a row, within sight of the other POWs, and beaten with bamboo clubs. The beating went on throughout the day, and included a mock execution. Then the men were made to stand to attention all night on top of a small hill. The following day the beatings continued. On the second night they were forced to stand to attention on the hill again. Every time they collapsed from pain and exhaustion the guards revived them with bayonets and rifle butts.

After the third night their ordeal was interrupted by an American air raid on the nearby Japanese airfield. The three gunners staggered to a trench to shelter. After the air raid the Japanese stopped the punishment, warning that any more attempts to get food would result in execution. All three men were close to death from their injuries and from dehydration and Gabbert had a broken arm. Patrick Aherne:

> Lance Bombardier Blyth, acting as [volunteer] medical orderly, persistently asked the Japanese Camp Commandant to dress it and was eventually allowed to do so despite the opposition by Japanese NCOs.

On Christmas Day 1943, the Japanese made the POWs a present of a horse's head. They skinned it, boiled it up, and made a stew. This was the first time anyone had had a full stomach for a long time. The New Year continued in the same grim pattern of hard labour and hunger; morale was low. Nolan sat on his blanket in the medical tent; as one POW described him, 'little more than a pile of skin covered bone'. He struggled to eat the tiny bowl of rice that made up the daily meal and sat waiting to die. Michael O'Connor tried to cheer him by talking about Ireland. But Nolan was losing the will to live.

By February 1945 only twenty-one POWs were still alive. They were all grievously ill with malaria, beri-beri, dysentery, and leg ulcers that ate flesh down to the bone. The POWs who were still working stole tiny amounts of food which they smuggled back into camp. This helped Nolan recover slightly, especially a tin of salmon that provided some much needed vitamins.

The POWs were moved to nearby Watom Island, which the Japanese considered vital in defending Rabaul from invasion. The men were employed digging tunnels to be used for communications and defences. They were split up into groups of four or less and taken away by whatever Japanese Army unit wanted them.

Captain Mallett, Gunner Hodson, and Gunner O'Connor were in their hut one evening. A drunken Japanese soldier, known as The Jockey, walked in. The Jockey was a groom who looked after a Japanese officer's horse. He was hated by the POWs because of his part in torturing Aherne, Fowler, and Gabbert, when they'd been caught trying to obtain food. The Jockey thrashed the three soldiers using a bamboo pole. Captain Mallett was especially vulnerable because he had huge ulcers on his legs which had eaten the skin down to the bone. Mallett died from his injuries the following morning. The other two, already weakened from disease and starvation, never recovered from the attack. Gunner Hodson died in May, and Gunner O'Connor died in June.[105]

When the Japanese government capitulated to the Allies, the eighteen surviving POWs on Watom Island were taken back to Rabaul. Their survival stood on a knife edge. Many Japanese officers still wanted to kill the POWs rather than allow them to be freed. On one occasion, before Australian forces arrived to take the Japanese surrender on Rabaul, the eighteen POWs were lined up in front of a machine gun to be shot. It was only the last minute intervention of a Japanese Colonel, plus a Japanese interpreter, Higaki, that prevented the men from being murdered.

Patrick Aherne and Patrick Nolan were eventually liberated by the Royal Australian Navy. Nolan remained in the British Army after the war. He died, in 1983, at the Royal Hospital, Chelsea.

After the eighty-two sick men had been left at Rabaul, the 'Gunner 600' main party were taken to Ballale Island. This group now consisted of 517 men: There were at least six Irish soldiers amongst them.[106] Not a single man survived.

The POWs built an airfield on Ballale by hand, labouring without adequate food or water in baking tropical heat. Starvation and disease took a lethal daily toll, while others died during air raids. Approximately eighty men were still alive in 1943. And these men were executed when the Japanese authorities thought that they might be liberated by Allied forces.[107]

Unknown to the Japanese, the Allies started to receive information about the men on Ballale as early as December 1942. Some islanders, who hated the Japanese Army, informed a Coastwatcher (one of the men who remained behind the lines secretly observing Japanese activity) that European POWs were working on Ballale Island.

The men were building an airstrip, as part of the Japanese preparations for invading Australia. It came under attack from Allied bombing. But the POWs were forbidden to use air raid shelters or trenches, and some were killed or wounded. An Allied pilot was forced to bail out of his damaged aircraft during one raid. A Chinese forced labourer witnessed what happened to the pilot:

> The Japanese tied his hands behind his back and made him sit on the ground; they put a drum of boiling water beside him and nine of them filed past, each one pouring a tin of boiling water over him, the man screamed in pain. I saw him fall flat on the ground, lie still and stop screaming, he appeared to be dead.[108]

Chinese witnesses testified that after air raids the Japanese guards would take out their anger on the POWs. A Chinese labourer described how he:

> … witnessed the Japanese pouring tins of boiling water over a prisoner and as they poured the water the man was screaming in pain and the Japanese were laughing and clapping their hands, some of the Japanese slapped the prisoner with their hands and some with sticks.[109]

By May 1943 there were approximately eighty POWs left alive on the island. The island was shelled by an American warship in June 1943. This was assumed to be the softening up bombardment for a landing. There was no subsequent landing; nonetheless, the Japanese murdered the remaining POWs. According to the witness statement of a Korean worker: 'I heard from the Japanese that the remaining POWs, about 70 or 80, were all killed; a big hole was dug and the POWs were shot and put into it.'[110]

After the war, the War Office (now part of the British Ministry of Defence) conducted an inquiry into the fate of the Gunner 600 party. For reasons which remain unclear, the War Office thought that the men had died onboard a ship bombed by American aircraft and were subsequently buried by the Japanese at Ballale. But Ballale Island was an Australian territory, and jurisdiction fell to an Australian war crimes investigation. They continued with an investigation into the British POW deaths which revealed the truth.

Ozaki Noriko commanded the Japanese construction battalion building the airfield. He was accountable, on a day-to-day basis, for the employment and welfare of the POWs. Admiral Kusaka Jimichi, the officer commanding all Japanese forces in that theatre of war, had overall responsibility for them. Both men admitted signing a defence plan, stating that all Allied prisoners on Ballale Island would be killed if there was an Allied attack.

The massacre at Ballalle is a clear reflection of Japanese policy. Similar plans, and practial preparations, such as the digging of mass graves, were later made throughout the Japanese POW camp system. A policy memorandum from the Japanese war ministry was sent to every POW camp in 1944, in anticipation of their liberation. Camp commanders were informed that it was intended that they should wait to act under superior orders before taking 'special measures'. But in the absence of such orders they ensured that no Allied POW left captivity. There is no ambiguity in the following:

> Whether they [the POWs] are destroyed individually or in groups, or however it is done, with mass bombing, poisonous smoke, poisons, drowning, decapitation, or what, dispose of them as the situation dictates [and] in any case it is the aim not to allow the escape of a single one, to annihilate them all, and not to leave any traces.[111]

12

RAILWAY OF DEATH

Two brothers, from Cork, lie buried at opposite ends of the Burma Railway. The eldest brother, Lieutenant Richard Duke, is interred in the beautifully tended Commonwealth War Cemetery at Kanchanaburi, Thailand. He died of a heart attack in May 1943, at Kannyu River Camp. He was only forty-four years old, still a relatively young man and not the most obvious candidate for a heart attack. But this was a common enough occurrence amongst POWs suffering from cardiac beri-beri.

Richard's younger brother, Private Basil Duke, lies in Thanbyuzayat War Cemetery in Burma. He died three months after Richard, in August 1943, at Sonkurai Camp. His POW records show the cause of death to be from tropical ulcers.

Richard and Basil Duke were two of the 13,000 Allied POWs who died implementing the Imperial Japanese Army's scheme to build a railway, linking Nong Pladuk in Thailand to Moulmein in Burma. Japanese ships were at risk of attack from Allied submarines, even in the early stages of the war when Japanese victories came thick and fast. A railway would shorten the sea journey, make it easier to supply the Japanese forces occupying Burma, and facilitate the removal of food and goods back to Japan.

A plan to build a railway linking Burma to Siam (Thailand) had been mooted by the British as long ago as 1887. The plan had been abandoned because of the difficulty in finding sufficient labour, and the dangers to them in cutting through the jungle and extreme terrain.

Work on the Japanese plan started in October 1942 and was completed by December 1943. The Railway was 264 miles long. In construction terms it was an impressive achievement. But the human cost was appalling. The exact number of fatalities remains unknown due to the lack of accurate record keeping, especially for the conscripted Asian civilians. An estimated 100,000 Asian forced labourers died from disease, starvation, and the effects of cholera, which swept through their ranks with the virulence of a medieval plague. The POWs fared better because they were part of a disciplined organisation that struggled to maintain hygiene standards and give medical care to the sick.

The Burmese end of the railway was started by Australian, British, and Dutch POWs transported from Java and Sumatra in Hellships. They travelled inside the holds of dilapidated merchant vessels in conditions akin to eighteenth-century slave ships. Many POWs died from heatstroke in the unventilated cargo holds, their situation worsened by the withholding of water, food and medical care.

The men who commenced work in Thailand were transported up from Singapore, and through Malaya, in cattle trucks. They were packed into unventilated wagons, without adequate water supplies or toilet facilities, during a four-day journey in equatorial heat and humidity. The stench inside a cattle wagon crammed with thirty men, some of whom invariably suffered from dysentery, is unimaginable.

On arrival in Thailand the men had to march to their section of the railway. As the railway progressed further, the journey proved longer and longer. Each work party usually had to construct their own camp in the jungle and build huts made of bamboo where they slept at night. The further away from the railhead the groups were, the worse the conditions became. It was harder to get rations to the more remote jungle camps, so the death rate from starvation increased. To pile misery on top of misery, the monsoon season brought a whole new raft of hygiene problems. And the Japanese guards generally forbad building effective toilet facilities, so the inadequate toilet pit latrines overflowed exacerbating cholera epidemics.

The actual construction of the railway was done mainly by hand. Japanese surveyors went ahead and marked the route. Teams of POWs followed along behind, clearing the jungle vegetation using hand-tools like axes and saws. They were followed by other POW work groups who built embankments, or dug cuttings out of the rock, creating a level plane for the railway track.

Earth embankments were made by POWs using chunkels (hoes) to dig up soil which was carried in bamboo baskets to the top of the embankment. Cuttings through mountain passes were carved out using sledgehammers on the loose rock, followed by blasting when bedrock was reached. Two-man teams, one man holding a long steel drill which the other hit with a sledgehammer, dug holes deep into the rock so that explosive charges could be laid.

Other POW teams built timber trestle bridges, 680 to be exact, across rivers, where men stood chest deep in water driving piles into the mud. The final act was the laying of the rail track on to the rail bed, by hand of course, with the rails bolted together and hammered onto the sleepers.

From an engineering perspective, the Burma Railway's construction is easy to understand. Comprehending the human cost of work on the railway is a more tenuous process. We live lives far removed from the grim realities of the POWs' struggle for existence. Listening, first hand, to a veteran's recollections, painfully brought back after half a century trying to forget, can be a salutary experience. But few of these men survive now. And many people interpret the Burma Railway and the whole tragedy of Far East POW existence from Hollywood's version of events, that is the Oscar-winning film *Bridge on the River Kwai*.

There really is a bridge over the River Kwai, though not quite as depicted by Hollywood. The Thais, eager to oblige, renamed the river that ran under the only remaining POW-built bridge to help the story fit together.

In 1942, Kanchanaburi was little more than a few dusty streets and tiny open-front shops surrounded by lush jungle vegetation. Today it's a small town with air-conditioned hotels providing a warm welcome for the hordes of travellers who come to see the bridge. Twice a day trains trundle across the bridge, taking tourists on day trips along the remaining operable track. The precautionary hand of the health and safety man hasn't reached the bridge so it is possible to walk across it. And if the train happens to cross at the same time, simply step to one side, taking care not to fall off the edge, and wait for it to pass.

People associate this bridge with the film, *Bridge on the River Kwai*, in which actor Alec Guinness plays the fictional Colonel Nicholson. In the interests of restoring his men's dignity and morale, Nicholson collaborates wholeheartedly in the building of the bridge. Later, a sabotage attempt is made by a Special Forces team inserted into the jungle. Nicholson spots the wires leading to the explosives planted under the bridge and reveals them to the Japanese. His betrayal results in the failure of the mission to blow the bridge and the death or capture of many of the sabotage team.

The film was based on a book written in 1952 by Frenchman Pierre Boulle. Boulle's personal wartime experience informed his book which was written as a work of fiction decrying the madness of war. He trained as a member of the Free French resistance, with Force 316, a British unit set up to undertake intelligence and sabotage missions behind enemy lines. Boulle also became a POW. But he was a prisoner of the collaborationist Vichy French regime. He was captured whilst travelling to Hanoi to meet up with Free French agents, and imprisoned for two years. So his own experiences, which undoubtedly scarred him, were suffered at the hands of his own countrymen and not the Japanese.

Boulle corresponded with former British POWs after the war and read published POW accounts, drawing upon their experiences to inform some of the incidents portrayed in his book. From this Boulle weaved a mixture of truths, half truths, and nonsense, into an entertaining work of fiction. This was seized on by Hollywood and made into a film portraying British soldiers efficiently and enthusiastically building a high-quality bridge for the Japanese and conspiring to protect it from Allied destruction.

Most former POWs were outraged by the film. The truth is that the River Kwai never existed. So there was no such bridge (though of course there were many others). The bridge over what we now call the River Kwai, since the Thai government renamed the river to make history and geography fit the whims of Hollywood, was built by soldiers under the command of Lieutenant Colonel Philip Toosey. Unlike the bridge in the film this is a steel bridge, though a temporary wooden bridge did run parallel to it during the war. The river running underneath it is, or rather was, the Khwae Noi. *Khwae* is Thai for river and *noi* means little. This 'little river' joins up with the Khwae Yai, the 'big river', better known as the Mae Khlong. The name 'Kwai' is simply a word meaning river that the troops picked up on during the war. Brave men died building the bridge over this river and many more would have died were it not for Colonel Toosey. Yet for many of the tourists, guide book in hand, and Hollywood nonsense in mind, the film is reality.

The site of the current bridge was known as Tha Maa Kham, a historical reference to a crossing place once used by an invading Burmese Army. Inevitably, the troops shortened the name to Tamarkan. At this time Kanchanaburi hadn't expanded to its present size, and the area around the bridge was little more than jungle. This was cleared to make space for a POW camp.

135 Field Regiment (Royal Artillery), commanded by Lieutenant Colonel Toosey, was sent to Tamarkan in October 1942, to join up with a larger force to build a bridge over the

river. The regiment had previously served in France and been evacuated at Dunkirk. Toosey led his regiment with distinction during the campaign in Singapore and was devoted to the men under his command. A measure of the man is that he refused an order to leave Singapore a few days before the capitulation, when ordered to escape to India and use his expertise to form another regiment.

Unlike the fictional Colonel Nicholson, Colonel Toosey didn't give a damn about the bridge. And unlike the film, conditions at Tamarkan were as grim as anywhere else on the Railway. Toosey did feel, however, that by negotiating with the Japanese he had a chance to obtain slightly better treatment for his soldiers. In doing this he showed his leadership and courage on a daily basis, standing up to the Japanese, despite the beatings it often earned him. The bridge was going to be built no matter what: The only difference that Toosey's negotiations made was reducing the number of POWs who died in the process.

The fictional Colonel Nicholson collaborates enthusiastically with the Japanese, believing that building the bridge will help to restore his men's *esprit de corps*. He even orders his officers and the sick men to assist the Japanese. In reality there was no attempt by any British officer to build the bridge in record time, or any other nonsense inferred by the film. Gordon Smale, a former POW who slaved on the Burma Railway, spoke from experience when he commented on the film to this author; 'British officers didn't behave like that – they just didn't behave like that.'[112]

Captain Ernest Gordon, an officer in the Argyle and Sutherland Highlanders, worked on the bridge. He described both book and film as an entertaining fiction. But he spoke for many when he complained that the film was an injustice to the men who built the bridge, unwillingly, at the point of a bayonet, whilst doing all they could to sabotage it.[113]

There were at least six Irishmen in Toosey's regiment. All of them survived their captivity and returned to Ireland. There were also numerous Irish soldiers from other regiments under Toosey's command at Tamarkan. One of them was Private William Carleton, from Wexford, serving in the East Surrey Regiment. He described Colonel Toosey as, 'a very brave officer and a good camp commander, [he] was often slapped in the face and stood to attention for hours outside the guard-room when he tried to save a man from getting a flogging.'[114]

Returning to the film, Nicholson actively tries, and fails, to prevent one of his men escaping from the camp. Of course, the heroic celluloid escapee is an American. But in the real world at Tamarkan, surrounded by jungle, and hundreds of miles from the nearest potential safety, escape was virtually impossible. There were successful escapes in Indochina, where men could blend in with and be assisted by anti-Vichy French residents. But in Thailand escapees died from disease and starvation in the jungle, were betrayed for monetary rewards by the Thais, or were re-captured and executed by the Japanese. Either way the usual result was an unpleasant death. Yet some brave men were determined to escape regardless of risk and Colonel Toosey helped them. Private Carleton described an attempt by four men from the East Surrey Regiment:

> This is how it came about ... Colonel Toosey was informed by the leader of the four before the escape ... and he [Toosey] said he'd do all in his power to help them. Each man had a bag of rice and some tinned food saved from our Red Cross [parcel] and they carried a compass and a diary of what had happened up to then as a prisoner of war.[115]

The four soldiers escaped at the same time as two officers, Lieutenant Howard and Captain Pomeroy. Carleton:

> The leader of the group, Private Duvall, told me that they planned to meet the two officers at a place somewhere he would not tell ... Every Sunday all prisoners crowded out

the gate of the camp to the nearby jungle to gather fire-wood. The weather was cold and the prisoners wore their blankets around their shoulders to keep warm. The four men wore their blankets around their shoulders which covered their load of supplies they carried. When they got into the jungle we said good luck and good bye.[116]

Colonel Toosey, at great personal risk, concealed their absence at roll-calls for three days. When the Japanese discovered the men were missing they called the Kempeitai in to investigate. They interrogated Toosey along with the soldiers from the same hut as the missing men. The men were beaten up by the Kempeitai. Private Carleton: 'After some days the Jap police came to question us about them. We said we did not know nothing.'[117]

The four soldiers were re-captured after ten days on the run. Warrant Officer Ivor Williams, from County Cork, was acting as temporary Camp Sergeant Major. He recalled that the soldiers, 'were caught by the Thai police and handed over to the Japanese'.[118]

Sometime after being brought back to camp, the four soldiers were taken into the jungle and executed after being made to dig their own graves. Private James Griffin, from Dungarvan, another East Surrey Regiment soldier: 'the men were believed killed by bayonets by the Koreans'.[119] Two weeks later, the two officers, who had been betrayed by Thais, were brought back to camp. The Japanese tortured them for three days, made them dig their own graves, and then bayoneted both men to death.

In real life (unlike the Hollywood version of the British POW experience) the escapees were British, and they were murdered for their efforts. The colonel and his soldiers did what they could to slow down progress on the bridge. The bridge was eventually destroyed by Allied bombing (note the replacement spans) and no one was happier about this than Colonel Toosey. Not quite the same story as the film …

After the Railway was completed most work camps were evacuated and the worst of the sick men taken in cattle trucks to the base hospitals on the southern end of the Railway. Conditions there were appalling by any normal standards, but far better than on the Railway construction camps. Rations were slightly better and anyone who had some money was able to buy extra food.

Red Cross supplies came in more frequently. According to Sergeant John Hazard, from Dublin, 'cigarettes, biscuits, peanuts, sugar, and coffee [came in] about every three months from the Red Cross in Bangkok'.[120] And whilst the Japanese and Korean guards continued to steal the POWs' Red Cross food, a creeping realisation that the war was going badly for them started to be seen in their attitude. Hazard: '[some of the guards] became friendly to the POWs and afraid of the Thais'.[121] But change, when it did come, was too late for many of the POWs.

The (nominally) fitter men were often employed looking after the sick. Geoffrey Scott Mowat arrived at H Force hospital camp, and discovered a number of friends, volunteer soldiers, who had all played bridge together in Singapore: 'Found Jack [John] McEvett, [from Dublin] a skeleton with malaria and dysentery, he died a few days later.'[122]

Two weeks later Arthur Prigge, a Trinity College graduate from Dublin, died in one of the nearby ulcer huts. Prigge normally worked in the Education Department of the Malayan Civil Service teaching mathematics. He was something of an intellectual and was rumoured to have written a book on bridge. Perhaps he hadn't been the most obvious candidate for the career of wartime soldier. Nonetheless, he'd joined the Straits Settlement Volunteer Force and had been captured at the fall of Singapore.

Another volunteer soldier, Paul Gibbs Pancheri, was being cared for in the dysentery hut by Geoffrey Scott Mowat. Pancheri described Arthur Prigge's death:

He … got into a desperate state with what, I suppose, must have been septicaemia, for his body was covered in ulcers, and no matter how each one was cleaned up, it would break out again, and a new one would start up next to it. In the end it became impossible to do any more for him. His awful ulcers were dressed and covered with leaves as no further bandaging was obtainable, and presently he died in dreadful misery. The ulcer hut in which he had lived had a pervading stench which can only be imagined.[123]

Watching friends die was a common occurrence on the Railway. Ten years after the war, the memories still searing fresh in his mind, Alfred Allbury wrote movingly about discovering Michael Duggan (from County Meath) in one of the dysentery huts at Tarsao hospital camp:

Mickey Duggan had been an old friend of mine … I had hardly recognised Mickey. The flesh had melted from his body, his skin was yellow, his eyes were sunk deep in their sockets and already as the hollows deepened around his mouth his teeth protruded like those from a skull … I sat numbed and quiet, thinking of the man I had known: Mickey with his trousers pressed, everything slick and neat and off to a dance in Stafford; Mickey who got all the girls, who bragged and laughed a lot, who was always in some scrape. He was only twenty three and soon he would be dead. He lay there with his eyes open but I knew he couldn't see me. There was no pain now, nothing hurt, nothing mattered … the blow flies crawled across his blanket … the bugs, the lice, the hard slats, the brassy sunlight, the pains in the stomach, the filth, squalor and slow misery of it all – they didn't bother Mickey now. Even as I sat beside him the paralysis of death crept into his eyes.[124]

The following day Allbury was a pallbearer at his friend's funeral. Michael Duggan was laid down on the earth whilst the Padre performed the last rites. Then his body was lowered into the ground. There was no coffin to dignify Gunner Duggan's interment. His body was wrapped in the same pathetic scrap of blanket that he had died in. It's a measure of the POWs' desperation that even this was valuable and had to be reused. So the Padre asked Allbury to recover the blanket.

Allbury, like all POWs, was no stranger to death. He jumped into the grave and pulled the blanket from his friend's corpse trying, in respect, to avert his eyes. But he didn't turn away quickly enough and found himself unexpectedly shocked by the sight that met his eyes:

A plug from an old khaki shirt was rammed into the mouth; two other plugs had been forced up the nostrils, there were activities after death that made these plugs a hygienic necessity. It was a skeleton that lay there, the skin taut over the arched structure of the ribs; the wrists bound together with a piece of string; the hands resting in the hollow that had been a stomach. How could this have lived, how could it have been, only a few hours before, someone I knew? It was a parcel of bones wrapped in yellow parchment. But it was Mickey. God, what suffering must a man have known that he became in death such a tragic indecency![125]

But as we walked away I looked at the sea of two thousand crosses and I wished that I had tears to shed for each and every one. But for two thousand deaths like the death that Mickey knew all the sorrow in the world could not atone.[126]

The Irish Prime Minister Éamon de Valera. Under his leadership Ireland remained neutral throughout the Second World War. However, many Irish men and women did join the Allied armed forces. (Wikimedia Commons)

Emperor Shōwa (Hirohito), who was Emperor of Japan during the Second World War. (Wikimedia Commons)

Above: Japanese troops entering Saigon, 1941. (Wikimedia Commons)

Left: Japanese troops on Bataan, Philippine Islands, *c.* 1942. Captured Japanese photograph. (Wikimedia Commons)

Above: HMS *Prince of Wales* in 1941, she was later sunk, along with HMS *Repulse*, off the coast of Malaya, near Kuantan. (Wikimedia Commons)

Right: HMS *Repulse*. (Wikimedia Commons)

Below: The Royal Navy heavy cruiser HMS *Exeter* sinking after the Battle of the Java Sea, 1 March 1942. (Wikimedia Commons)

This picture, which was captured from the Japanese, shows American prisoners using improvised litters to carry those of their comrades who, from the lack of food or water on the march from Bataan, fell along the road. Philippines, May 1942. (Wikimedia Commons)

FEPOWs on the death march from Bataan to Cabantuan Prison Camp, May 1942. Note that the prisoners have their hands tied behind their back.

The Bridge over the River Kwai, Kanchanaburi, Thailand, part of the Burma Railway which was built by the Japanese using POW slave labour. (Mjanich, Wikimedia Commons)

Kanchanaburi War Cemetery, Thailand, where many of the POWs who died during the construction of the Burma Railway are buried. (Niels Mickers, Wikimedia Commons)

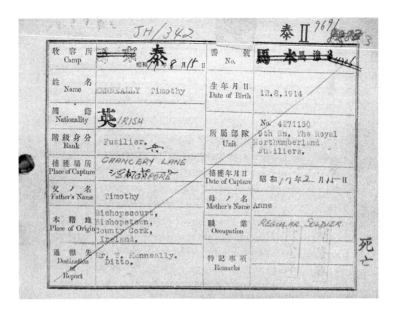

収容所 Camp	泰 昭和 ? 年 8 月 15 日	番 號 No.	
姓 名 Name	KENNEALLY Timothy	生年月日 Date of Birth	12.8.1914
國 籍 Nationality	英 IRISH		No. 4271150
階級身分 Rank	Fusilier.	所屬部隊 Unit	9th Bn. The Royal Northumberland Fusiliers.
捕獲場所 Place of Capture	CHANCERY LANE SINGAPORE	捕獲年月日 Date of Capture	昭和 17 年 2 月 15 日
父ノ名 Father's Name	Timothy	母ノ名 Mother's Name	Anne
本籍地 Place of Origin	Bishopscourt, Bishopstown, County Cork, Ireland.	職 業 Occupation	REGULAR SOLDIER.
通報先 Destination of Report	Mr. T. Kenneally. Ditto.	特記事項 Remarks	

死亡

Above and below: Fusillier Timothy Kenneally's POW index card. Kenneally was unlawfully executed by the Japanese after attempting to escape. The reverse of the card (below) states in English that he was 'caught on March 23 and was disposed of'.

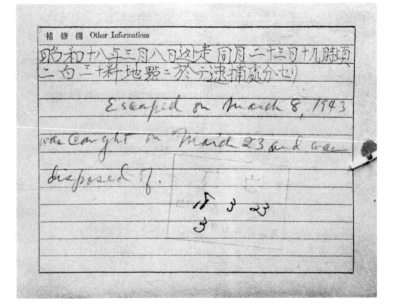

補修欄 Other Informations

昭和十八年三月八日逃走同月二十二日乃十九时頃
二句三十粁地點ニ於テ逮捕處分セリ

Escaped on March 8, 1943

was Caught on March 23 and was
disposed of.

18 3 23
3

Right: A replica of the Old Changi Prison Chapel at the Changi Museum, Singapore. The chapel was originally constructed by Australian and British prisoners of war (POWs) in Changi Prison in 1944. At the end of the war it was dismantled and shipped to Australia, where it was put into storage. It was reconstructed and unveiled in 1988 in Duntroon, Canberra, as a POW memorial. The same year, a replica of the chapel and a museum were built in Singapore next to Changi Prison. When Changi Prison later expanded, the chapel and museum were relocated to a new site a kilometre away and were officially reopened on 15 February 2001. (Whoosises, Wikimedia Commons)

Below: Nurses rescued from Los Baños POW camp, March 1945. Chief Nurse Laura Cobb is speaking with Admiral Thomas Kinkaid. (Wikimedia Commons)

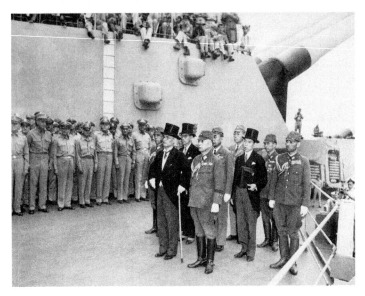

Japanese surrender signatories arrive aboard the USS *Missouri* in Tokyo Bay to participate in surrender ceremonies. (Wikimedia Commons)

The defendants at the International Military Tribunal for the Far East Ichigaya Court: Accused Japanese war criminals in the prisoners' box. Front row of defendants from left to right: General Kenji Doihara; Field Marshal Shunroku Hata; Koki Hirota, former prime minister of Japan; General Jiro Minami; General Hideki Tojo, former prime minister of Japan; Takasumi Oka; General Yoshijiro Umezu; General Sadao Araki; General Akira Muto; Naoki Hoshino; Okinori Kaga; Marquis Koichi Kido. Back row: Colonel Kingiro Hashimoto; General Kuniaki Koiso; Admiral Osami Nagano; General Hiroshi Oshima; General Iwane Matsui; Shumei Okawa; Baron Kiichiro Hiranuma; Shigenori Togo; Yosuke Matsuoka; Mamoru Shigemitsu; General Kenryo Sato; Admiral Shigetaro Shimada; Toshio Shiratori; Teiichi Suzuki. (Wikimedia Commons)

13

AN IRISH CRUCIFIXION?

Some men felt that trying to escape was worth the likelihood of torture and execution. After all, they were dying from disease and starvation anyway. One group escaped from Tha Kilen, a camp on the Burma Railway, in March 1943. Two of the men were Irish, Fusilier Timothy Kenneally, from Bishoptown, and Private Patrick Fitzgerald, from Kilmeadon. The third man, Sergeant Francis Joseph Kelly, was possibly Irish, or Liverpool Irish. The fourth member of the group, Sergeant Edward Reay, was English.[127] Witness accounts of their escape attempt and subsequent execution differ slightly over small details and specific dates. This is not surprising though as the POWs were not allowed to keep calendars, diaries, and writing materials.

Sergeant Kelly managed to obtain and keep hidden a number of escape items. If they had been found in his possession he would have been executed. Corporal Thomas Finn, from Mitchelstown, County Cork, was serving in the 1st Battalion Manchester Regiment. Kelly asked Finn to join his escape group, in January 1943. Finn:

> [Kelly] told me that he was going to make an escape and wanted … [me] to accompany him. He had medical supplies, tinned fish, and concentrated soups, also firearms (revolvers). We turned down the offer for the following reasons; no map, no compass, [and] as we were proceeding further up country with the Japs, when we reached top camp it would be time enough to start then.[128]

Corporal Finn never did 'start then'. Perhaps it was a wise decision, as he survived his incarceration and was liberated in 1945. He may have been put off by one of the many brutal executions staged by the Japanese in order to deter escape attempts. Finn:

> During the real hard times at Prankasi, an Australian, Private McCarthy, was brought in by a Thai. After several beatings they placed him on a platform on a high tree tied hand and foot and left him there for three days. He suffered so much from malaria he was eventually placed in hospital. [Later] they came for him and took him onto the railway. We heard a rifle volley. Later the Jap party returned to camp laughing. We could never find the body or the grave.[129]

Sergeant Kelly escaped along with Kenneally, Fitzgerald and Reay. Finn:

> I heard that Kelly eventually made the attempt but was caught and brought back to Chungkai and shot. Many knew of the execution but nobody seems to have seen the dead bodies.[130]

The four men escaped from their camp at Tha Kilen on the night of 6 March 1943. They remained at large for around two weeks until apprehended by Thai policemen. Seemingly they shot one Thai policeman who tried to capture them, but were later caught and overpowered by more Thai police.

An Australian surgeon at Hintok, Lieutenant Colonel Dunlop, saw the men on 25 March. They were being taken back by lorry to their own camp to be executed. According to Dunlop they had been captured after being betrayed by the Thai people who were supposed to be guiding them.[131]

Japanese evidence given at a post-war War Crimes Tribunal, states that the four men were executed, 'on or about 27 March

1943'.[132] A senior British officer (and former POW) described it bluntly 'as the murder of four British prisoners of war on 30 March 1943'.[133] Joseph Fitzgerald's POW record card claims that, 'we [Japanese] chased him and shot him to death on 23 March 1943'.[134] Similar comments are found in the Japanese records of the other three men. Kenneally's record has the interesting addition: 'We arrested him for the time being on the fourth of March, 1943. However he tried to escape again during the investigation on 23 March. So we shot him to death.'[135]

Many Japanese POW records were written with an eye to covering up war crimes. Sergeant George Priestman gives a more compelling account of the death of the four soldiers, in a sworn affidavit, written after the war:

> About the 27th of March, 1943, we were quartered outside the Main Camp, and about 7.30am I saw four British soldiers … escorted by 32 Korean guards who were armed with rifles. The Camp Commandant was with them, together with two other Japanese officers. The party crossed the Railway line out of our sight. At 8.45am I heard a volley of shots nearby and immediately afterwards were five or six ragged rifle shots. Three or four minutes later I heard three revolver shots at intervals of a second or two.[136]

An hour later, Sergeant Priestman, with some other POWs, walked across the railway line to a nearby Japanese rifle range. The sight that met them was, to put it mildly, disturbing. Priestman:

> In the undergrowth nearby we found three bamboo crosses, about seven feet by four feet. We also saw another bamboo cross jutting out of the ground. We uncovered it and found the dead body of a British soldier, tied to the cross with his arms outstretched. He had been shot. Nearby there were three mounds of loose earth. We did not uncover these

mounds, but built up four proper mounds and placed small bamboo crosses on top.[137]

These were the bodies of the three Irishmen and their English comrade.

Sergeant Priestman said that the uncovered body they found was still tied to a cross. He did not describe it in these words but one (or more) of the soldiers may have suffered some sort of crucifixion prior to death. Now this could have been merely a convenient way to secure the man whilst the Korean soldiers were shooting him. But why go to the trouble of making a cross. Thirty-two soldiers can easily shoot an unarmed man where he stands, or simply tie him to a tree before shooting him? Why did they leave one corpse on view, but hide the other three?

There is documented evidence that the Japanese crucified POWs elsewhere. For instance, the following statement was made to a post-war Australian War Crimes Tribunal. It is an eyewitness account of a crucifixion, at a camp in Sandakan, described by a Chinese cook who was hiding behind a hut:

> The Jap officer [Nishigawa] stood on the stool with the hammer in his right hand. He then raised the prisoner's left arm and driving a nail through the palm of the left hand fixed it to the left arm of the cross which was the height of the prisoner's shoulders ... the prisoner tried to wriggle and scream whereupon Hinata [another Japanese officer] held the body of the prisoner against the upright post of the cross and put a piece of cloth in the prisoner's mouth. The Jap officer ... then nailed the prisoner's right hand to the cross in the same manner. He then ... nailed both of the feet of the prisoner with two nails to a horizontal board on which the prisoner was standing.[138]

The Japanese officers continued to torture and mutilate the POW until finally, 'the Jap officer took a knife and cut a piece of flesh from the prisoner's right hand side … he then put on a rubber glove and pulled out the prisoner's intestines which were placed on a wooden board.'[139]

The Japanese officer held responsible for the deaths of Kenneally, Fitzgerald, Kelly and Reay, was Lieutenant Colonel Yanagida Shoichi. He was charged with 'committing a war crime … in violation of the laws and usages of war'. The usual response to such charges was twofold. First, that they had no knowledge of the Geneva Conventions and second, that escaping POWs were treated according to the same rules that Japanese soldiers were. Unimpressed by this response, a War Crimes Tribunal sentenced Yanagida to twenty years imprisonment.

14

A HELPING HAND AND A LISTENING EAR

Japan, finding itself with a large pool of potential labour, wasted no time in making the best of this new resource. Employing POWs in safe occupations, such as agriculture, not directly linked to the war effort was an internationally accepted convention. In Great Britain, for instance, German and Italian POWs were given the option of employment on farms, which many chose to do. But there were strict rules governing their conditions of work, which were more favourable than those given to British civilian farm workers. In fact, quite a few German and Italian POWS liked it all so much that they stayed on after the war ended.

The Geneva Conventions, which had been signed though not ratified, were not complied with by the Japanese and POWs working for the Japanese were not accorded with the rights and treatment they were due.

The one advantage of working for the Japanese was that it gave the POWs a chance to sabotage the Japanese war effort. This was the POWs' opportunity to wreak revenge on their enemies and they seized it with enthusiasm. Indeed, there were factories in Japan, employing POW slave labour, where the POWs later claimed that no properly functioning machine ever left the factory. But getting caught committing sabotage was a guarantee of torture or even death. Nonetheless, according to Sergeant Peter Horan, RASC, from Dublin, 'sabotage was rife in almost all camps'.[140]

Prisoners were sometimes forced to clean and maintain Japanese weapons. This was contrary to the Second Geneva

Convention and all normal customs and usages of war. So the POWs turned it into an opportunity for sabotage. Gunner Christopher Alston, from Dublin: 'while cleaning small arms for the Japanese, [I] destroyed ejection springs[141] on Light Machine Guns.'[142] In effect this would cause the weapon to jam when fired – a potentially fatal occurrence if it happened in combat. Gunner William Barter, from Dublin: 'While unloading bombs and detonators from [trains] at Tamuang on the [Burma] Railway I threw a lot away into the jungle [and] in Singapore I filed down the firing pin of the Japs' rifles while cleaning them'.[143]

POWs were often used on larger weapon projects. Sergeant Walter Barker, from Tuam, Galway, was one of a mixed British, Australian and Dutch work party forced to construct anti-aircraft gun platforms at Bangkok airport. Supervision, whilst usually brutal, was often technically unsophisticated. Most guards were (former) peasants with limited education. So, when Japanese engineers left the POWs to be supervised by Japanese and Korean guards, the POWs took advantage of their lack of knowledge. In this instance Barker, and the other POWs, deliberately used the wrong mix when mixing concrete and the weakened gun positions collapsed when the heavy guns were placed on them.

Michael Lynch, from Charleville, worked at various sites throughout Singapore during 1942. He was a Royal Artillery driver. As the Japanese had a serious shortage of drivers and mechanics, they made some POWs drive and maintain their vehicles. Lynch and other members of his unit took every opportunity to damage Japanese MT vehicles. They were assisted by Chinese mechanics, who hated the Japanese Army following the slaughter of thousands of (Singapore) Chinese civilians. Gunner Lynch: 'We were helped on this [sabotage] work by Chinese and Eurasian mechanics who were doing sabotage of their own at the same time. They were all civilians who had previously worked with the RAF and RAOC.'[144]

POW labour was used at the docks in Singapore, right up until liberation in 1945. Gunner William Ivory, from Dublin, was imprisoned in River Valley Camp, Singapore: 'Most of the men from this camp worked on the docks unloading ships. We damaged and destroyed as much as possible, such as aeroplane parts, machinery and motor lorries. Many of us got beaten up by the Japanese, myself included.'[145]

On rare occasions, a POW might get a chance to damage far more than machinery. John Kenneally, a merchant seaman from County Cork, reported that a Royal Navy rating, 'Able Seaman Cox, killed a Jap whilst working – dropped timber on his head.'[146] Working also gave opportunities to steal food. It might be eaten there and then or smuggled back into camp. Private Thomas McGrath, from Ballymartin, rose to the occasion magnificently. McGrath (2nd battalion The Loyal Regiment) was sent to Korea on one of the Hellships, the *Fukkai Maru*. Then he was taken by train to Mukden POW Camp, in Japanese occupied China, arriving in November 1942.

McGrath was an old soldier. He had enlisted in 1931 and had previously served in Palestine. He used the skills and ingenuity that career soldiers generally acquire, to damage the Japanese war effort and help himself and his pals. McGrath: 'I was working in the foundry where I was able to destroy small parts which were important for several special machines. I also sold 900lbs of silver sand to the Chinese for money to obtain food for myself and other prisoners.'[147]

Indeed, the machine tool plant at Mukden, where the POWs were used as slave labour by the Japanese Mitsubishi Corporation, rarely managed to produce a fully functioning machine throughout the war, thanks to the efforts of the POWs.

Another task that McGrath put his skills to was obtaining newspapers, 'I was one of the few who could obtain newspapers from the Japs and Chinese ... I took them to camp where they were read by officers who understood Japanese.'[148] News, the progress of the war, helped to sustain morale, and whilst Japanese newspapers were heavily censored they often reported German reverses quite accurately.

In Thailand and Burma, and elsewhere, a clandestine network of radios kept the POWs informed of the progress of the war. Radios, or wireless sets to use the terminology of the time, played a vital role in maintaining morale. News of victories spread throughout the camps, as the tide of war turned against Japan.

The Japanese were aware that wireless sets were being used and constantly sought to locate them. And if caught the wireless operators could expect to be interrogated, tortured, and then executed. Sergeant John Caddy, from Kildare, recalled, 'the courage of those British personnel, who, at various camps, maintained a radio news service knowing full well the dire penalties if discovered.'[149] In Java, Sergeant Vincent Slavin, from County Donegal, was one of a group of five men, 'working a broadcast receiver – all members of the Royal Signals.'[150]

Soldiers from the Royal Signals often operated the secret radios as they had the training and knowledge to do so. However, there was much more involved than this. Radios needed a power supply. Ingenuous hand-operated generators were sometimes used, but numerous POWs risked their lives smuggling batteries past the guards into various camps.

Surgeon Commander Vincent Walsh, from Ballina, recalled the ingenious way one radio was hidden. Walsh had been the doctor onboard HMS *Exeter*, famous for its part in the sinking of the German cruiser *Admiral Graf Spee*. But *Exeter's* luck ran out in March 1942 when she was sunk during the Battle of the Java Sea. Walsh became a POW and helped with the operation of an illicit radio: 'Whilst a POW at Batavia in 1944 I had a wireless set working in my billet. I was the senior officer in charge.'[151]

The hut contained a mix of British and American officers, plus an American civilian called Buchanan. Walsh:

Buchanan, a civilian, formerly in the US Navy, put the set together. It was in a pair of clogs. He had a wooden leg and [later on] he used to transport the set in it. He was employed by SPWRY [sic] bomb sight firm in Singapore. [In Batavia] he had the set in a stool which I carried from one part of the camp to another, passing a Japanese sentry on one occasion.[152]

15

'THEY WERE A WALL UNTO US ...'

Former FEPOWs can be scathing and sometimes bitter about their respective governments and some of their officers. But there is one group of whom, with very rare exception, every POW spoke of with nothing but gratitude and praise: the medical staff.

Hundreds of doctors, medical orderlies, nurses, and medical technicians, went into Japanese captivity. The Imperial Japanese Army also confiscated large quantities of drugs, and medical stores, from the Allied military hospitals and medical units.

Japan could have provided effective medical care to every POW, at absolutely minimal cost and effort to themselves. Instead, the Japanese deliberately created insanitary conditions, leading to mass epidemics and illness, and then watched whilst Allied soldiers died, refusing to release drugs, or even vitamins, from storage. They hoarded medical equipment, forcing British and Australian doctors to operate on injured soldiers, performing amputations and other major surgery without anaesthesia, using home-made scalpels. In short, Japanese policy caused medical problems that directly led to the death of thousands of POWs.

In 1945 when Japan surrendered, their camp administration finally released hoarded medical supplies. In one camp the British medical officer, Doctor Hardie, reported how they handed over large quantities of atebrin (for malaria treatment), iron, vitamins, and Red Cross Money. All this, and various other drugs and medical items, had been kept locked away in a store whilst POWs had been dying from their lack.[153]

Of course, conditions varied. At Changi, and the so-called base hospitals on the Burma Railway, facilities were a little better. Doctors had simple equipment and some drugs, often smuggled in at great risk from outside camp. In the more remote camps men died in agony in vermin-infested bamboo huts with little more than the love and prayers of their comrades.

Squadron Leader Aidan MacCarthy, from Cork, was one of the many Irish doctors serving in the British armed forces. He had previously been evacuated from Dunkirk, with the British Expeditionary Force, when the Nazi blitzkrieg over-ran France. After Dunkirk he was posted to Java and eventually captured when Japanese forces over-ran the island. Doctor MacCarthy described POW food as appalling, consisting of dirty unwashed rice and a few half rotten bits of vegetable. Despite this, they shared it out with the precision that only starving men can understand. This diet led to vitamin and pro-tein deficiency diseases. One ingenious response to this was to provide vitamins with yeast drinks made from pure yeast, obtained by trading outside the camp.

Doctor MacCarthy's description of an attempt to provide protein for sick POWs makes the stomach heave. But it's a measure of the POWs' desperation that they were forced to these extremes:

> The rice ration ... was heavily infested with rice weevil. These ... floated to the surface when the rice was cooked. They were then creamed off and boiled separately to pro-duce 'maggot soup' which, after straining, was served to the sick as a form of protein addition.[154]

The rice issued to the POWs was nothing like the clean, white produce familiar to most of us today. It was invariably the rot-ting sweepings of the factory floor fouled by and with every kind of vermin. MacCarthy:

Dirty rice produced other unpleasant products besides maggots ... it also contained earthworm eggs and these often hatched out in our stomachs, and in two occasions in the lungs of POWs. From the stomach the hatched worm proceeded up the passage from the stomach to the throat and then crawled into the nose or mouth. I have seen a man playing bridge ask to be excused for a moment, remove a worm from his nose or mouth, and then return to the table. Nobody took any undue notice.[155]

Contaminated food and water also caused widespread dysentery: one of the major causes of death. Flies vectored bacillary and amoebic infections. The concomitant dysentery was the by-product of these infections, with inflamed mucous membranes of the large intestine, resulting in foul diarrhoea laced with the patient's own mucous and blood. This decimated men whose immune systems were already weakened by starvation.

In a few camps doctors were able to build stills and produce saline solution which they used to intravenously re-hydrate dysentery cases using needles made from bamboo. Ingenious and desperate measures like this saved lives in those camps where the Japanese allowed it. But this was often not the case. MacCarthy:

One particularly grim memory I have is that of a dying airman in the dysentery hut. He was in the terminal stages of acute bacillary dysentery, and had not long to live. Because of the severe abdominal cramps and pains it is a most painful way to die. His wasted body stiffened with each spasm and he had no controls over his bowels and bladder. There was little or no medicine to be had and all that I could do for him was to pray and hold his hand and whisper words of encouragement ... as the airman weakened a guard came into the hut. I did not notice him and therefore failed to give him the routine ... salute. The guard, having thus 'lost face', rushed towards me screaming with his rifle raised. In a hurried mixture of Japanese, Malay and English, I tried to explain that the patient was dying. In fact, ironically, he died during our altercation. The guard knowing he was in the wrong, hesitated. But as I turned back towards my prostrate patient, the guard smashed his rifle butt onto my right elbow and fractured all the bones in the joint.[156]

Far East POWs suffered from so many medical problems that too conscientious an account would end up looking like a medical textbook. Some of the most common illnesses were dysentery, malaria, tropical ulcers, cholera, and beri-beri. MacCarthy:

Beri-beri ... was due to a deficiency of the vitamin B complex in our diet. This disease produced a variety of symptoms, the commonest being an acute burning sensation in the feet and scrotum combined with severe leg cramps and leg muscle wastage. This was the dry form of beri-beri. The wet form was less common and caused swelling of the ankles, scrotum and abdomen. Both led to the heart being enlarged on one side with resulting breathlessness. The vitamin deficiency also caused retrobulbar neuritis, an inflammation of the ends of the optic nerve in the eye ... which if untreated ... led to permanent blindness.[157]

Irish soldier Tim Finnerty had beri-beri, whilst imprisoned in Burma. He frequently had to watch his comrades suffering from this illness, as they slowly walked around the prison compound waiting to die. With wet beri-beri, the patient retained water until the lungs and heart became so swollen that death resulted from heart failure which happened to Private John Kelly, from Dublin, a soldier in the Manchester Regiment. In the dry form the patient became doubly incontinent and gradually wasted away to skeletal thinness and death.

Beri-beri was the cause of death of Dubliners, John Keelty and John O'Connor; and Thomas Hare and Wilfred Theakston, from Cork; and so many other men, too numerous to mention.

Parasites thrived on and inside the wasted bodies of men weakened by starvation and forced into insanitary living conditions of medieval ilk. Diseases of the skin, bowels, ears and eyes were rife. Perhaps one of the most common ailments was tropical ulcers, described with a professional eye by Doctor MacCarthy:

> Tropical ulcers were another widespread affliction … initially they were caused by an insect bite which itched, was scratched, became infected, ulcerated, and, owing to the low physical state, became chronic. In each case, dirt, sweat and inadequate dressings (which were often in the form of a piece of paper or a large leaf held together with a piece of string), contributed to a continuous suppurating series of ulcers which ate deeper into the flesh, often reaching the underlying bone and causing it to become infected – a condition known as osteomyelitis.[158]

The usual treatment for ulcers was to scrape out the necrotic flesh, without anaesthesia, using the end of a teaspoon. Some men recovered, some died. Private Basil Duke, from Cork, and Private Arthur Prigge, from Dublin, both died from tropical ulcers, as did many other Irish soldiers.

The medical staff suffered from the same ailments as POWs did, yet at the same time they took on the self-appointed role of protectors of the sick and, quite literally, stood between their patients and the Japanese. Sapper Edward Brehony, from Sligo, was working at Kanu (Tarso) on the Burma Railway, in October 1942. He commented on the courage of Captain McNeilly, the medical officer:

> My medical officer prevented, in defiance to Japanese orders, sick men from working – risking punishment in

doing so. I saw him beaten and tied to a tree for a similar act and [he] took punishment like a hero. I saw this officer giving every possible medical attention to sick men whilst he himself suffered from severe dysentery and malaria.[159]

Lance Sergeant Thomas Smith, from Cobh, County Cork, worked at Kanu Camp in November 1942. He also commented on the actions of Captain McNeilly and other medical officers: '[There were] constant protests by doctors, who were often punished by slapping, at general living and working conditions in camp. Also, despite Japanese threats, they refused to allow (as far as possible) sick men to work.'[160]

It needs to be understood that repeated slapping as practiced by the Japanese Army was a procedure of such violence that men might be left with missing teeth or a broken jaw. Captain Alfred Olson, a Dubliner serving in the Royal Army Ordnance Corps, worked on the Burma Railway. His praise for the work of one medical officer is unequivocal:

> The conduct of Captain Phillips RAMC [Royal Army Medical Corps], whilst Senior Medical Officer at Hintock Valley Camp, Siam, deserves notice. A very sick man himself, almost blind from vitamin deficiency, his work was an example to all. Many lives were saved solely by his cheery and sympathetic manner. Drugs were practically non-existent. Cholera and dysentery were rife in this camp. I owe my life to this officer.[161]

Illnesses associated with starvation and nutritional deficiency thrived in all Japanese POW camps but certain diseases, like cholera, were worsened because of the location. Cholera is caused by a bacterial infection. With effective medication and medical care cholera is unpleasant, but rarely fatal. Untreated, the symptoms are agonising. Violent diarrhoea and vomiting cause rapid and severe dehydration and weight loss. The body is racked by excruciating abdominal cramps and death often occurs within hours. When properly treated less than one per cent of cholera patients die; amongst POWs the mortality rate from cholera was as high as 50 per cent.

Cholera broke out along the Railway during 1943 with the coming of the rainy season. Like the rain itself, it was completely predictable. Cholera always accompanied the rains in Thailand at that time. But now it spread like wildfire amongst the thousands of unvaccinated debilitated prisoners, whose sanitary facilities provided the perfect medium for infection.

Japanese and Korean camp guards, and railway personnel, were contracting cholera and suffering losses too. So the Japanese administration finally provided anti-cholera serum to *some* of the POWs on the Railway. But dozens and dozens of Irish soldiers, too many to list here, contracted cholera. To make matters worse, the cholera outbreak overlapped with the Speedo period. In order to speed up the completion of the Railway, the Japanese forced the men to work even longer hours. And they made sick and dying men come out of their bamboo hospital huts to work on the Railway.

Flight Lieutenant Frederick Parke, from Dublin, was originally captured in Java. He was sent to Hintok Valley Camp in Thailand in May 1943 and remained there, as one of the medical officers, until December. Parke:

> I was continually over-ruled by the guards as regards the fitness of men for work. It was an almost everyday occurrence for the sick personnel to be paraded and made to do work for which they were quite unfit to do despite my protests to the contrary. On one occasion, Engineer Officer Hirota ordered a hundred extra men to be made to work. These men were taken from the hospital. The majority of these men struggled back from the work in a deplorable condition ... in my opinion the deaths of many of the prisoners was hastened as a result of being forced to work when unfit to do so.[162]

Parke had been sent to Hintok as part of the ill-fated H Force. He left Changi on 5 May 1943 with an advance party of 400 men. They went by train for five days, in rice trucks, and then marched from Bampong (Thailand) to Hintok. The men staggered along 100 miles of dirt tracks through the jungle, stopping at filthy maggot-infested staging camps *en route* where they were forced to bargain with Thais to buy drinking water. They were in such a poor physical condition that only twenty-seven of the 400 men actually reached Hintock, despite the efforts of Japanese and Korean guards who flogged even the sickest men onwards with bamboo sticks.

The men who managed to reach Hintock were eventually joined by the remainder of H Force: around 3,000 men in total. But H Force was only one of a number of POW groups who went up the Railway, and Hintock was only one of many camps. For instance, there was a workforce of 1,600 British POWs at Songkurai; 1,200 of these men died from the effects of the Speedo and cholera.[163] Padre Duckworth, speaking from experience, described Sonkurai as the horror hell of Prison Camps. Duckworth was also moved to pay tribute to the medical staff there, including Dr Hutchison, from Waterford, who was known with affection as 'Hutch'.[164]

Death on a mass scale presented funeral challenges beyond the capacity of the survivors. Hasty mass graves were sometimes unavoidable. But normally the POWs made every effort to bury their dead in formal, dignified, burial services, led by a Padre, when one was available. The Japanese attitude to POW funerals was unpredictable. Sometimes they would ridicule or even forbid religious burial services, yet on other occasions they would show respect to men whose unnecessary deaths they had just caused and pay full military honours.

When deaths were due to cholera, the Japanese and Korean guards usually stayed well clear. Though at Hintok (Railway camp) a Japanese officer was so keen to see one POW buried that he beat him with a shovel and pushed him into a grave.

Then he tried to force a POW burial party to fill the grave in whilst the victim was still alive.[165] In this instance the unfortunate man was rescued by the POWs, who refused to bury him alive despite being violently beaten by Japanese guards.

Most cholera victims were burnt, immediately and without ceremony, in an attempt to limit the spread of infection. At Songkurai Private Patrick Carberry (from Dublin) had the grim task of disposing of the bodies: 'Myself, Corporal Hulley, and Corporal Mackenzie, both of the Manchester Regiment, did the job of cremating the bodies of the POWs, who died of cholera at Songkurai, by burning them.'[166]

Carberry also acted as batman to Captain James Mudie, the officer in charge of cremations. The Japanese ensured the cholera area was isolated from the main camp, and they kept well clear of it. In civilian life Mudie worked for the Malayan Broadcasting Corporation and he had helped to smuggle a secret radio from Changi when they were sent up to the Railway. Now Mudie made good use of the isolation to operate the radio and pass on daily news bulletins to the main camp.

They were nearly caught out on one occasion when the Japanese decided to spring a surprise search. The POWs, however, had procedures in place to respond to this and the camp bugler blew the officer's mess call. Unknown to the Japanese, this was a warning that a search was starting. Normally the radio was hidden away. But Mudie had slipped up and left the set unattended in his hut. The Japanese would assuredly have found it during the search, and the likelihood is that Mudie would have been tortured and executed. Carberry, hearing the warning bugle call, threw the wireless set down a borehole just before the search party walked in.[167]

Private Carberry was one of the few POWs to leave Sonkurai alive. Before he left, he burnt the corpses of four of his countrymen. Private William Burke and Private Alfred Davidson, both from Dublin, were cremated on the 30 May 1943. Private Thomas Higgins, from County Kildare, died of cholera on 4 June 1943. He went into the flames the following day, along with Andrew Boyd from County Cork.

Disease and illness also killed doctors and RAMC medical orderlies, at the same time that the need for their services increased. Volunteer medical orderlies stepped into the breach. Sergeant Ron Thompson recalled the actions of Leading Aircraftsman Paddy McQuade, a medical volunteer on the tropical island of Haroekoe:

> Within days of arrival, dysentery swept through the ill-prepared camp. Work was suspended and bamboo/attap huts were built for the sick. If one was admitted to No. 1 Ward, it virtually meant a death sentence for the patient. Word went round for volunteer medical orderlies to nurse the living skeletons, racked with pain, bereft of friends and often longing to be relieved of their mortal toils. Although no medical man, Paddy possessed the ideal qualities needed for such a harrowing and demanding job; limitless patience, courage of the highest stamp to perform the many gruesome tasks, compassion, the ability to encourage men to fight to hold on to life and a no-nonsense adherence to his Roman Catholic faith.[168]

Moved, as only those who have looked at death and watched the best and worst in men can be, Ron Thompson completed his eulogy:

> Paddy miraculously survived the Haroekoe experience and, at the end of our captivity, became ill in Sumatra at the Pakanbaroe base camp ... three weeks after the Japs capitulated, our saintly little hero, whose only possessions at the time were an old enamel bowl, a spoon and a rosary, sank into his final sleep and bade farewell to a world which had been all the richer for his life and good works.[169]

Lieutenant Colonel Frederick McOstrich, from County Tipperary, recalled the courage of another volunteer medical orderly. Signalman Tonge was caring for a group of POWs who were being moved by rail to another camp. The Japanese Army never moved POWs under the protection of the Red Cross, which was meant to be prominently displayed on transport carrying POWs or wounded men. Instead, they moved POWs in unmarked trains and ships, which then appeared to be legitimate targets to Allied air and naval forces. McOstrich:

> When the Thai-Burma Railway was subject to severe bombing a train containing POWs was heavily bombed and machine gunned. Signalman Tonge was in charge of the sick and throughout the bombing carried stretcher cases to a place of safety until he himself was killed. This gallant action was reported to me when the remains of the party arrived in my camp.[170]

Other soldiers risked their lives to care for sick and dying POWs by trading with the local people. According to Lance Corporal Philip Farrelly, from Louth, there were always men, 'breaking past guards and [the] wire for the purpose of bringing in food and drugs bought from the Thais.'[171]

In Batavia, Corporal Michael O'Donnell (RAF), from Rathkeale, was in a section of the camp where the men were separated from the officers. O'Donnell, who was ill, praised the bravery of an RAF medical officer who took tremendous risks to help both him and other sick POWs:

> Flight Lieutenant Tierney [from Cork] was continuously agitating for extra medical supplies from the Japs. Although our section of the camp was out of bounds for him, he broke through barbed wire fencing to bring us [medical] supplies, nearly every night for about a fortnight, until he persuaded the Japs to admit us to [the prison camp] hospital.[172]

Alongside dedicated medical care, another factor played a part in keeping men alive – a robust sense of humour. Servicemen are renowned for having the ability to laugh at themselves, and at each other, and seeing the funny side of situations that civilians might well see as only tragic.

Ron Mitchell was a Singapore Volunteer, as were a number of Irish soldiers. At Kanu Camp, on the Railway, he was one of a large group of men being glass rodded (cholera tested). This humiliating procedure, where a Japanese medical orderly shoved a glass rod up each POW's anus to obtain a sample was endured stoically by most of the men. Though one man, a chartered accountant in civilian life, and rather more sensitive than most of the soldiery, bent over in front of the doctor but refused to pull his buttocks apart. The long line of naked POWs were cheering and laughing. Mitchell:

> The [Japanese] doctor got off his chair and … shoved the rod right up Dom's bum. He let out a wounded roar and leapt forward about three feet. There was a tremendous roar of laughter and even the Japs joined in. The final humiliation was Dom being called back to have the rod removed. Later the Japs produced a supply of cholera vaccine and our doctor, Major O'Driscoll [from Skibbereen], was to do the inoculations. There must have been about two hundred of us and the Major had his own style. None of this bedside rubbish like putting the patient at ease … his style was to throw the syringe like a dart. The single needle was blunt at the start of the proceedings; heaven knows what it was like at the end.[173]

16

HMS *JUPITER* AND HAROEKO ISLAND

HMS *Jupiter*, a Royal Navy destroyer, was serving in the Mediterranean in November 1941. Then she was detached from the Mediterranean Fleet, to join the destroyer escort accompanying HMS *Prince of Wales* and HMS *Repulse* to Singapore.

HMS *Prince of Wales*, HMS *Repulse*, and attendant destroyers (Force Z) left Singapore on 6 December and sailed north to confront a Japanese invasion fleet. HMS *Jupiter* stayed behind in Singapore because of mechanical troubles. After repairs, *Jupiter* escorted evacuation ships away from Singapore. Then she was in action against a Japanese submarine, which she sunk with depth charges during a surface action in which some of *Jupiter's* crew died.

On 27 February 1942, HMS *Jupiter* took part in the Battle of the Java Sea, a desperate last ditch attempt by a small Allied fleet to stop a vastly superior Japanese invasion force from getting to Java. Following an inconclusive long-range engagement with some Japanese destroyers, *Jupiter* hit a mine and sank.

There were two young Irishmen onboard HMS *Jupiter*: Ordinary Seaman George Pringle, from Galway, and Ordinary Seaman Paddy Quinn, from County Kildare. In an interview with the author, former crew member Harold Lock recalled his own experiences as a sixteen-year-old boy: 'Oh yes, I remember George Pringle', he said. Then he continued describing the last hours of HMS *Jupiter*:

> About an hour after we had broken off the action [against the Japanese ships] – while I was on the stern of the ship

acting as a loader in a gun's crew – we hit a mine. The ship
was sinking and we got the order to 'Abandon Ship'. I swam
towards the shore [of Java] and soon after daybreak I heard a
voice in the water close by. It was one of the boys from my
ship. He told me that sharks had got quite a few of our crew
and the Japs had shot several men in the water.[174]

Exactly how many men reached the shore is unclear: Japanese
patrols killed a number of survivors and then rounded up the
remainder, including Pringle and Quinn. Harold Lock and his
friend were exhausted when they crawled up onto the beach.
A group of Japanese soldiers stood there pointing their rifles
at the boys. Lock: 'A [Japanese] sergeant produced two spades
and told us in sign language to dig two holes. Then he lifted his
rifle to show that he intended to shoot us.'[175]

Whilst digging their own graves they heard a voice speaking in American-accented English. The Japanese soldiers stood
to attention and the boys looked up to see a Japanese officer
watching them. He explained (in English) that he had spent
some years living in America. Then he ordered the soldiers not
to murder the two boys. Lock: 'I will never forget him. He was
the only Japanese I ever met who showed even the slightest
hint of compassion.'[176]

They were taken a few miles along the beach to join a group
of prisoners, including eighteen other survivors from HMS
Jupiter. Lock: 'The Japs took any watches or rings or anything
we had. Our officer asked for some food for us. And they beat
him up really badly – knocked him down – kicked him.'[177]

After around four weeks sleeping under guard in a jungle
clearing, four POWs died from starvation and disease. Then
the group was taken to Batavia and housed in a former school.
A few weeks later all *Jupiter*'s survivors were gathered together
in one camp. They were used as working parties, unloading
Red Cross parcels. These supplies were intended for the prisoners. But the Japanese Army immediately confiscated them.

The death toll amongst the POWs was rising. So when the Japanese told the men that many of them would be moved to an island, where there would be light work and plenty of food, most of the men from HMS *Jupiter* were pleased to be going along. Of course, they suspected that the Japanese were lying. But they thought that anything had to be better than their present situation. How wrong they were …

After a seven-day voyage they reached the island of Haroekoe,[178] a name that was to become a byword for brutality, even by the standards of the Japanese POW camps. They landed on Haroekoe in April 1943. Lock:

> When we arrived there was no huts, nothing, we just had to lie down in the rain. We had to build our own huts and after about a week the Japs made the natives help us as they knew how to build huts [from attap] a lot quicker than we could. Then the Japs took us about a mile away and said they wanted a runway built.[179]

Forcing sick men to construct a runway with little more than hand tools, in the tropical heat, without food or even sufficient drinking water was a criminal act. The results were predictable. Lock: 'Straightaway men started dying but they [the Japanese Army] kept bringing more men in by ship.'[180]

One of these replacements, Airman Peter Handibode, from Westmeath, died and was buried in a communal grave. Lock:

> Nobody wanted to volunteer to dig the graves because we didn't have the strength. By then I think I weighed something like about five and a half stone. We used to dig a hole in the mornings, we'd put in as many bodies as we could in them, sometimes as many as ten bodies in one hole – we'd cover them up with layer and layer of dirt, that's all.[181]

This might sound callous or indifferent. But the men in this POW camp were traumatised walking skeletons, numbed by daily familiarity with death, disease, torture, starvation and misery. It wasn't that they didn't care, but for now they just had to survive; caring could come later. And after the war the bodies (including Airman Handibode's) were dug up and re-interred with full honours in Ambon Commonwealth War Cemetery. Harold Lock:

> Four prisoners tried to escape, but they were reported to the Japs by some natives when they tried to get a boat from them. They were brought back to the camp and shot. We were all forced to witness this. But death had become so commonplace that we were getting like robots without feeling anything except wanting to cling to life.[182]

Sergeant George Till (RAF), from Dunraymond, also tried to escape, along with two friends, Leading Aircraftsman Jelly, and Sergeant Bailey. Till: 'We made three or four attempts but had to abandon them being unable to get a suitable boat. The 12th of September 1943 was our best opportunity. But returning back to camp after a recce [reconnaissance] we were nearly caught by a sentry.'

One of the men knocked something over in the dark, making a noise, and the men ran back to their billets. What happened next isn't known, though it's safe to assume the men weren't caught as Till was sent to Batavia soon after this. But escape attempts and clandestine night-time reconnaissance were the exception, not the norm. The daily routine continued. Lock:

> We were woken every morning by the guards, often by blows with a stick. We had a handful of rice and maybe a banana if we were lucky. Then we were marched to work with the fitter prisoners helping the weaker men who

often collapsed. Then when our daily work was finished we
walked back to camp and got another handful of rice.[183]

The death toll from starvation and dysentery continued to rise,
worsened by the Japanese and Korean guards using the POWs'
water supply as a latrine. The Japanese moved some of the
worst of the sick POWs from Haroekoe to Java in the latter
part of 1943. On 24 November a large group of men, many
of them on stretchers, were packed into the hold of a filthy
coal barge. The following morning they set off on a short but
unpleasant journey to Ambon. A few POWs died *en route* and
the guards threw their bodies overboard.

The POWs arrived in Ambon, around midday on 25
November, and were immediately transferred to another ship,
the *Suez Maru*. The ship was carrying wounded Japanese soldiers in holds 1 and 2, and the Haroekoe POWs were packed
into holds 3 and 4. The following morning another group of
POWs, from Ambon, was put into the hold with the Haroeke
men. Most of the stretcher cases were left on deck next to the
hatches leading into the holds. The guards did this to make it
quicker to throw the bodies overboard when the men died.

The *Suez Maru* sailed from Ambon on 26 November 1943,
heading for Surabaya, with around 550 POWs onboard.[184] On
the morning of 29 November the *Suez Maru* was intercepted
by an American submarine, the USS *Bonefish*, near the Kangean
Islands, north of Bali. By this stage of the war most Japanese
naval codes had been broken, enabling the Allies to intercept a
significant amount of Japanese shipping. Despite this Japanese
ships rarely displayed the internationally recognised markings
indicating that POWs were onboard. So the *Bonefish*'s captain
had no way of knowing that POWs were onboard.

At 8 a.m. the *Bonefish* fired a number of torpedoes at the
Suez Maru. One torpedo hit the stern near hold 4, killing or
wounding many POWs. The ship's engines were wrecked
and she gradually started sinking. The Japanese crew and the

Korean guards launched the lifeboats and rafts, but reserved the boats for themselves. Then those POWs who were able to get out of the holds jumped into the water. The remainder drowned inside the ship, as it finally sank, about an hour and a half after being hit.

A Japanese minesweeper, that had been escorting the *Suez Maru,* picked up Japanese and Korean survivors from the water. The captain of the minesweeper and the senior officers rescued from the *Suez Maru* were then faced with a dilemma: What should they do about the 200-300 Allied POWs in the water, clinging onto debris or kept afloat by lifejackets?

Minesweepers are relatively small naval vessels, and this one was full and unable to take anyone else onboard. They could have sailed away though and left the men in the water. But army standing orders forbade any action that might result in POW survivors being rescued by Allied vessels. And the USS *Bonefish* was still in these waters and the Japanese were worried that she might later return. So Lieutenant Koshio ,the Japanese officer in charge of the POWs, and a detail of one machine gunner and twelve riflemen, spent two hours shooting every single man in the water.[185]

Back on Haroekoe, work continued until July 1944. Then the Japanese moved the surviving POWs either to Amboina, or to Java. Over half of the original 2,070 men taken to Haroekoe in April 1943 died before the Japanese surrender in 1945.[186] Harold Lock survived and so did his Irish shipmate, George Pringle. Paddy Quinn, the other Irishmen from HMS *Jupiter,* died in October 1944 (probably) at Muna, in the Celebes.

17

THE GREAT ESCAPER

Japan had demanded military access to (Vichy) French Indochina in 1940. They used it as a springboard, bringing the Japanese Air Force within striking distance of Malaya. The Vichy administration was allowed to retain ostensible control over internal affairs. Then in March 1945, Japan took full control of Indochina.

In most POW camps the jungle, tropical diseases, and the physical isolation hundreds of miles from the nearest safe haven were more effective barriers than the thickest prison walls. But French Indochina was different. The sizeable French population gave an escapee some possibility of blending in and remaining unnoticed. There was also a degree of sympathy for the POWs, amongst some French civilians.

There were many escape attempts from Indochina, mainly from what is now Vietnam. Some were successful, most were not. According to Signalman Wilson, who attempted to escape from Saigon, the risks involved, if re-captured, were well known to the POWs:

> In Saigon, two British gunners, Cassidy and Baxter, 3rd Heavy AA Regiment, were caught escaping, brought back to camp [and] beaten in the guard room. Screams were heard by the lads in Camp. Later [the] Japanese informed those in camp that both men had been shot for trying to escape.[187]

Captain John McQuilllan, from Dublin, arrived in Saigon three months before Cassidy and Baxter were murdered. He commanded the Hospital Camp where he struggled with all the problems that doctors faced elsewhere. Though, in Saigon, the food and accommodation was better than in most of the Japanese POW camps. Rowley Richards, a doctor in the Australian Army, arrived there after a nightmare journey from Thailand by railway cattle-truck and then ferry. He was impressed both by the standard of the accommodation and by the warm welcome from Captain McQuillan, who he remembered from Singapore. In turn, McQuillan was visibly shocked by Richard's appearance and he immediately took him away to get some food.

Working on the docks in Saigon gave an opportunity to steal food, and the overall health of the POWs there improved. There was also a source of assistance that became a lifesaver. McQuillan: 'A group of French people secretly helped us throughout the three and a half years we were at Saigon ... This group, at considerable risk to themselves, kept us supplied with essential drugs, news, and money.'[188]

The resistance group also helped some men to escape. McQuillan: 'Gunner Purcell escaped from Kanoi Camp, Saigon, helped by the same people.'[189] In fact, Michael Purcell, an Irishman in the 3rd Heavy AA Regiment, escaped three times. He finally reached Allied lines in an amazing series of adventures that read like a novel.

Purcell distinguished himself earlier in the war, when he was separated from his regiment during the evacuation of the British Expeditionary Force from Dunkirk (France). He had disguised himself as a French Railway Engineer and travelled through the German lines to rejoin his unit at Dunkirk. The ability to speak French helped him then, and it would do so again during his daring escapes from the Japanese.

Purcell had joined the Royal Artillery in August 1939, just before the outbreak of war, and was promoted to Sergeant by the time he was captured in Singapore. He went into Changi POW camp along with thousands of others. But he wasn't moved to the Burma Railway where escape was virtually impossible. Instead, fortune favoured him and he was sent to Saigon in July 1942.

His camp, like many Japanese POW camps, was poorly constructed and he was able to slip through the wire and make contact with French and Annamite (Vietnamese) civilians. Purcell secretly broke out of camp numerous times, pretended to be a Frenchman, and bought desperately needed medicines for the camp hospital.

During one trip he made contact with Monsieur Goddard, a member of the De Gaullist resistance. Goddard hid a suit of civilian clothes in preparation. Then, when the escape route was ready, Purcell broke out again on 1 November 1944. Purcell: 'I went straight to the café Simon Petri in the Rue Saint Judel … I was conducted immediately by car to a house in Rue MacMahon where I slept the night. The enemy conducted a search the following morning in many houses of the city.'[190]

Purcell was collected by the (French) Chief of the Dockyard Police, Monsieur Tistanier, and his daughter. They were both supporters of the Free French De Gaullist movement. They took a massive risk in helping Purcell, as the Japanese would have killed them if found out. Tistanier hid Purcell in the boot of his car and took him to a mental asylum, where the chief doctor hid him for three nights. Then they smuggled him by car, for 317km, to Phan Thiet, in what is now south-eastern Vietnam. They left Purcell in the care of another French policeman for three more days. Purcell:

Tistanier [then] took me to a railway station at Phan Rang. Here I boarded a Japanese troop train and was told to contact a Frenchman on the train. When the train left I was in a carriage with some Japanese and Annamites,[191] dressed in the uniform of a French Railway Engineer … I travelled to a station 200km from Kang Ngei, got off the train and two Frenchmen came up to me and said 'Allez Messieurs' [a pre-arranged code]. I went through the gates, passed the Jap sentries in the midst of these Frenchmen, boarded a French military car which was already waiting and was conducted to a house in Kang Ngei.[192]

Purcell met the head of the Indochina De Gaullist movement – introduced only by the codename Number 42. The following day he took Purcell to a small French military outpost at Gi Lang[193] and left him there. Purcell: 'I was warned not to try an individual escape as the natives would kill me. I obeyed these instructions but nobody seemed to come to take me away. I was here until the end of January [1945].'[194]

This was wise, if frustrating, advice. The local Annamite people, often pro-Allied, but violently anti-French, sometimes struggled to differentiate between the two. But something soon happened to force events. Purcell, 'About 1st February, some American Airmen came to the post. They had force-landed in a seaplane at Tam Kam point. There were ten of them, the eleventh escaping in a submarine with French assistance.'[195]

Purcell and the Americans were taken by car to Ki Non to be picked up by a submarine. But the submarine *rendezvous* was cancelled and they were driven to an airfield at Pleiku instead. They waited, growing increasingly anxious, for a Douglas Dakota transport which was being despatched from Kunming (China) to collect them. Then the Japanese started fighting against the Vichy French on 9 February and the airport was rendered inoperable.

The group took to the jungle, moving between various French outposts and keeping one step ahead of the Japanese. Their plan was to head to the coast and try to make contact with a submarine. They reached Tu Non[196] in early March, but were divided as to the best route to take from there. So the group split up. The Americans, led by Captain Stevenson, went off with the French agent Number 42. Purcell accompanied another De Gaullist agent to Feifu.

Purcell was intercepted by the Japanese at Feifu. He put his knowledge of the French language to good use again and pretended to be a soldier in the French Foreign Legion. The Japanese believed him initially. However, they became suspicious and, imagining him to be an American airman, took him to Tourane for questioning. Purcell:

> I was beaten up, interrogated, accused of having bombed a Jap hospital ship – still as an American – and told I was to be shot next morning. That night at 2300 hours I got out of my prison and made for the river. I still had an American Army knife with me, strapped between my legs, and this fortunately had escaped detection. [Using the knife as a tool] I eased the bricks out of the wall and moving by the buildings escaped without being seen.[197]

Purcell ran to the river, crossed, and headed towards the sea. The following day he was caught by a group of twenty or thirty local people. They took him by sampan along the river, and then by road, and handed him over to the Japanese. This time Purcell succeeded in convincing the Japanese that he was in the French Foreign Legion. After being on the run for so long he was thin, debilitated, and suffering from the effects of malaria. Still thinking him French, the Japanese left Purcell in a French hospital in Hue.

Two months later, Purcell was put in a POW camp with French troops newly interned by the Japanese. Purcell:

> On 13th August, the Japs were marching us towards Savanakhet. There was a party of 500 including myself and a French NCO who knew the route. We escaped on the outskirts of Savanakhet, about 1900 hours, while we were having a break. Although there were numerous guards, we made off through the fence without being seen and made for a place called Phone Sime where there were believed to be native troops friendly to us.

Purcell met up with Laosienne irregulars in Laos, then part of French Indochina. They gave him food, clothing, and a guide to take him to meet up with French guerrillas. They then made radio contact with Allied troops in southern Laos, who were searching for POWs thought to be in the area. A Major in the Thai Army helped pass Purcell across the border into Thailand. Eventually he reached the HQ of the advance British Airborne Troops, under Colonel Smiley, at Ubon.

After three escapes from Japanese custody, an epic journey through enemy-occupied towns, and dense jungle wilderness, he eventually returned to the British Army in the final hours of the Second World War. According to the MI9 agents who de-briefed Purcell, he, 'showed resource and plenty of courage and daring'. They recommended that he should be awarded a decoration for bravery.[198]

18

BATTLE FOR HONG KONG

The Japanese Army occupied Canton in October 1938, in one more stage of a brutal war of conquest that eventually cost the lives of an estimated 20 million Chinese civilians. This left Hong Kong surrounded by Japanese forces and extremely vulnerable to attack. An eleven-mile series of linked defensive positions, the Gindrinkers Line, stretched from Gindrinkers Bay to Port Shelter. But no one imagined it capable of repelling a Japanese attack, given the overwhelming force they were able to bring to bear.

Recognising this, in 1940 the British government decided to leave the forces defending Hong Kong at little more than symbolic levels. This decision was reversed in September 1941, with the aim of bolstering Chiang Kai Shek's resistance to the Japanese and two Canadian infantry battalions were added to Hong Kong's British and Indian troops.

The assault on Hong Kong, like the attack on Pearl Harbour, was a surprise attack, made without any declaration of war. It started at 8 a.m. (local time) on 8 December 1941, when the Japanese Army invaded the (mainland) New Territories. The Japanese attacked with a three to one superiority, using 52,000 veterans of the war in China.

Hong Kong's garrison was 14,000 strong, including RAF personnel and the reservists of the Hong Kong Volunteer Defence Corps (HKVDC). On the first day of the campaign the handful of RAF aircraft, at Kai Tak, were destroyed on the ground by Japanese bombing and two of the navy's three destroyers were withdrawn to Singapore. Their loss, if they remained at Hong Kong, was inevitable given Japanese air superiority and their vulnerability to aerial attack.

On 10 December, two days after the initial assault, Japanese troops breached the Gindrinkers Line at the Shing Mun redoubt. The evacuation from mainland Kowloon started the following day. By 13 December, the last Commonwealth soldiers, men of the Rajputs (Indian Army), had left Kowloon and landed on Hong Kong Island. The island's defences were split into two brigades, East and West. Two days after the withdrawal to the island, Japanese artillery started to bombard the defenders, who rejected two Japanese demands that they surrender. Then Japanese forces crossed the narrow dividing waterway and landed on Hong Kong Island on 18 December.

The garrison put up a fierce, gallant resistance against overwhelming force. Inevitably, various small outposts surrendered when cut off and further fighting became pointless and suicidal. But a series of atrocities, notably at the Silesian Mission and the Sai Wan battery, where prisoners were murdered after surrendering, were a pointer for worse to come.

By 20 December the garrison was divided in two, with resistance concentrated around the Stanley Peninsula and the western side of the island. Ammunition, food, and water supplies were becoming perilously short and on 25 December the Governor of Hong Kong surrendered Hong Kong to the Japanese Army, to prevent the inevitable massacres which would have accompanied further resistance. This was a sensible and humane decision. Despite this, the Japanese occupation was stained by the wholesale murder of thousands of Chinese civilians and the deaths of many of the garrison.

For the soldiers, weary after weeks of brutal, often hand-to-hand street fighting, the surrender was a day of mixed emotion made more poignant by it happening on Christmas Day. The Imperial Japanese Army celebrated victory in its customary manner, murdering defenceless civilians and POWs during the confused hours after the fighting finished.

Many of the military hospitals became places of slaughter. Victorious Japanese troops rampaged through the wards bayoneting wounded soldiers in their beds. Nurses were raped and, in some cases, beaten to death. One of the foulest of these episodes occurred a few hours before the formal surrender of the garrison. Japanese soldiers captured the hospital at St Stephen's Green College. Amongst other barbarities they tied a group of young nurses on to a 'bed' of piled up corpses and gang raped them.

The Chinese civilian population fared even worse than the troops. Many were shot or bayoneted to death. Others escaped across the bay to the doubtful safety of the mainland. During the first few days after the surrender, British, Canadian and Indian soldiers were being brought in from positions around the island. Some men took advantage of the confusion to escape to China. One Irish soldier used his nationality to his advantage:

> Staff Sergeant Paddy Sheridan was working in the bakery (he was a baker). He was asked to produce his ID [by the Japanese who clearly did not realise he was a soldier] and an escort was sent with him to collect it. Sheridan concealed his Army ID and instead produced an Irish passport which was in Gaelic. The Jap officer could not understand it and took it away for examination. Some days later a very polite and humble Jap asked to speak to him and told him that as Ireland was neutral, he was free to leave the colony.[199]

Jesuit priests helped Sheridan to get a ticket to Macau – then a neutral Portuguese colony. He made his way from there through Japanese occupied China and across the border to Kunming, in Nationalist China, where there was an American air base. Of course, if the Japanese had realised that Sheridan was in the British Army his Irish passport would have counted for nothing.

There were many genuine neutral civilians resident in Hong Kong and naturally they asserted their rights to be treated as such. Neutrality had provided them little real protection during the Battle for Hong Kong. Though after the surrender, the Japanese treated neutral citizens with some degree of restraint.

Sergeant Harry Smith (Royal Naval Dockyard Police) and his son Signalman N.L. Smith (HKVDC) were both captured and imprisoned. Sergeant Smith later died in a POW camp in Japan. Sergeant Smith's wife and daughter escaped internment by the Japanese as they were Irish. They continued living in their house in Fung Fai Terrace, assisted by the International Red Cross. Mrs Smith eventually died from cancer. Her daughter Muriel, married to Bill Cameron, a policeman interned in the civilian camp in Stanley, remained at large.

Civilians (non-Chinese) were initially concentrated in various hotels and public buildings. Then the Japanese moved them to a collection of buildings near Stanley Gaol, designated Stanley Internment Camp. Many of the Chinese soldiers, of the Hong Kong Volunteer Defence Corps, took off their uniforms and blended in with the Chinese civilian population. The remaining Chinese HKVDC, along with their European comrades, joined the RAF and the British regular soldiers in Shamshuipo.

Prisoners moving into Shamshuipo faced a scene of devastation, caused during the fighting and subsequent looting by civilians. Rotting dead bodies lay around awaiting burial. Doors, windows, and every item of furniture had been removed. Only the empty shells of buildings remained, promising nothing but hardship and discomfort. British Indian Army troops were put in Ma Tau Chong, and the Royal Navy and Canadians were imprisoned in a former refugee camp at North Point. In all camps the immediate problems were the same: organisation had to be restored, wounded and dying men cared for, and the accommodation made as habitable as it could be under the circumstances.

Not surprisingly, minds turned to thoughts of escape. With nearby China occupied by the Japanese Army the chances of success were slim. Nonetheless, the Japanese required all POWs to sign a declaration promising not to try to escape. Most men signed knowing that declarations made under duress had neither legal nor moral authority. But some men from C Company of the Middlesex Regiment flatly refused, even after being tied up for hours facing the muzzle of a machine gun.

19

SAILING TO THE RISING SUN

POWs from Hong Kong were fed into Japanese industry via a series of shipments by sea. The first draft sailed from Hong Kong onboard the *Shia Maru*, on 4 September 1942. It consisted of 618 men, mainly from the Middlesex Regiment, the Royal Artillery and the Royal Scots, plus some from the Royal Navy. Collectively, they were known as the hard men.

The Japanese selected the men who had refused to sign the no-escape declaration for the draft. British officers were then forced to select the remainder. So they chose men who were known to be tough and who were, sometimes, a disciplinary problem. A number of officers, NCOs, and medical staff were also included.

There were plenty of Irishmen amongst the hard men, including Sergeant Herbert Morgan, Lance Corporal John Burke (Cork), and Edward Brennan (Dublin).[200] Regardless of their aversion to discipline, many of the hard men had distinguished themselves in the final days of the Battle for Hong Kong. Their toughness showed in the fact that, despite the poor conditions on the voyage, only two of them died and the group's mortality rate in Japan, whilst dreadful *per se*, was the lowest of all the drafts sent there from Hong Kong.

A merchant seaman witnessed their arrival at Kawasaki POW camp (Tokyo) a little less than two weeks after they left Hong Kong. His comments provide a telling reflection on the health and treatment of the Hong Kong POWs, given they describe men the Japanese considered fit for hard labour:

They were in a deplorable condition when they arrived, suffering from beri-beri, pellagra, scabies, ringworm, pediculosis, lice, acne, malaria, haemorrhoids, and ear diseases. They had many deaths from dysentery and diphtheria, and as medical supplies were so short they had to cut cards for who should have anti-diphtheria serum.[201]

The hard men were dispersed amongst different camps, mainly around Tokyo and Yokohama. For the remainder of the war they continued, as best as they could, to live up to their reputation. They proved to be mixed blessing to the Japanese war economy, committing acts of sabotage whenever possible. Edward Brennan: 'At the Railway when unloading any war materials, we would make sure it could not be used again.'[202]

Brennan survived the war, as did most of the Irish hard men. Herbert Morgan died in Japan, in February 1945, a few months before the end of the war. John Burke died in September 1945, when the aeroplane taking him home crashed.

There were six major shipments of POWs from Hong Kong. None of these voyages were pleasant. But the voyage of the *Lisbon Maru* easily merits the description of hell on earth. Quite some time after the *Lisbon Maru* disaster, when the final death toll was fairly accurately known, British Foreign Secretary Anthony Eden made an official statement to parliament:

A transport called *Lisbon Maru* was used to convey over 1,800 British prisoners of war from Hong Kong. On the morning of 1st October, 1942, the vessel was torpedoed by a submarine. The Japanese officers, soldiers and crew kept the prisoners under the hatches and abandoned ship forthwith, although she did not sink until 24 hours later. There were insufficient lifebelts and other safety appliances onboard. Some of the prisoners managed to break out and swim to land. They were fired on when in the water. In all at least 800 prisoners lost their lives.[203]

A report sent from the British Embassy, in Chungking, a few weeks after the sinking, lacked the dignified restraint of Eden's comments in parliament. Though it summarises events with grim candour: 'The vessel did not sink for 24 hours after the torpedoing, and the callous brutality of the Japanese in leaving so large a body of men battened down to drown like rats is beyond description.'[204] There were at least twenty-two Irishmen amongst them.

Their ordeal started, on 25 September 1942, when they mustered on the parade ground at Shamshuipo POW camp for embarkation to Japan. The Japanese wanted to transport 2,000 fit men to Japan to work as slave labour. There were around 4,000 prisoners left in camp by then. Many of them were suffering from diphtheria, dysentery, beri-beri and pellagra. All of them were starved and emaciated. There were few genuinely fit men left and the British officers had refused to nominate anyone to go to Japan.

In response, the Japanese selected 1,865 men they considered fit for work. Of these supposed fit men, thirty-one had to be carried to hospital before the ship sailed. The remainder were taken on-board the *Lisbon Maru*. The ship was a 7,000-ton freighter launched in 1920. Captain Kyoda Shigeru commanded the ship, and an army officer, Wada Hideo, commanded the Japanese Army guards. Another Japanese Army officer, Niimori Genichoro, who had lived in the USA, and spoke English, acted as interpreter.

Lieutenant Colonel Stewart, from the Middlesex Regiment, was the senior British officer onboard. Though, as another officer put it:

> One cannot say that Colonel Stewart was in command of the 1,800 men, except by his soldierly example and by the respect in which he was held [by the soldiers] for his dogged

retreat, against eight to one odds … during the defence of Hong Kong … The person in command was a brutal, callous Japanese interpreter named Niimori who had lorded it over us in the POW camp for the last nine months.[205]

The *Lisbon Maru* sailed from Hong Kong on 29 September. In addition to the POWs, the *Lisbon Maru* also carried around 700 Japanese soldiers. The ship had two eighteen-pounder Quick Firing guns mounted fore and aft. Most importantly, the ship did not display markings indicating that it was carrying POWs. In appearance, she was an armed merchantman, carrying Japanese troops, and a legitimate target of war. Two days later she was torpedoed by a United States Navy submarine, the USS *Grouper*, off the coast of Zhoushan (China).

Warrant Officer Fallace, a former Police Inspector from Tientsin serving in the Hong Kong Royal Naval Reserve, survived the sinking and escaped from the Japanese. He described events in a report written two months later:

At about 7am, on the 1ˢᵗ of October, [the] Japanese were heard running about on deck and at the same time shouting. Suddenly the vessel slewed to port [left] and we immediately received a crash on the port side aft. The ship shuddered for three or four seconds. By this time the Japanese had manned their guns and were firing … at the same time all men including the sick on deck were chased down into No. 1 hold.[206]

Number 1 hold already contained around 300 men, including most of the Royal Navy personnel. There were four men from Cork amongst them; Robert Hosford, James Kearns, Bartholomew O'Sullivan and Jeremiah Casey. Of the four, Casey was the only one to survive.

Conditions down below had been bad enough prior to the submarine attack. Warrant Officer Evans, who escaped with Fallace, described them:

There was a raised wooden platform, about 3 feet 6 inches in height, in the 'tween decks of the hold. The men were divided in two. Half slept above the platform and the other half underneath. The platform had to be entered by crawling on hands and knees with just a few inches above a man's head if he sat upright.[207]

Aside from being extremely unpleasant, the cramped conditions had obvious implications in terms of the men's health. Fallace:

The accommodation was considerably overcrowded, and when sleeping, men had bodies touching and legs overlapping … [also] at least 75% of the draft had some sickness or other, among which prevailed dysentery, diphtheria, beriberi, pellagra, [and] many had diarrhoea and very bad skin diseases.[208]

The situation was destined to get even worse. The Japanese battened down the hatches above all the holds. No food or water had been issued since the day before and the prisoners were sick, hungry, and dehydrated. Many of the men with dysentery were losing bodily fluids rapidly. For the sickest men, the denial of water was a death sentence.

There were medical personnel in each hold. Surgeon Lieutenant Jackson, from Limerick, was in No. 2 hold along with a few non-commissioned medical assistants. They did their best to care for the sick men. But without drugs or equipment they were fighting a losing battle.

As the day progressed the POWs could hear the sound of the Japanese getting the ship under tow from another vessel. It was seen as some reassurance that the vessel was not sinking. But during the afternoon they heard the towrope snap. Then the Japanese guards, on the deck above, blocked the small air chute leading into the hold leaving the men in total darkness. Fallace:

From this time on the air became absolutely foul and together with cries and moans from the sick all night the situation became unbearable. About 1 a.m. the first man died. Signals were then tapped in Morse through the bulkhead to Number 2 hold asking them to inform Colonel Stewart of the situation in Number 1 hold. Shortly after [this] the second man died.[209]

An officer in No. 2 hold listened to the tapping and translated the message for Colonel Stewart. But the situation in No. 2 hold was no better than in No. 1, with nearly 1,100 men crammed into a dark fetid space too small for even half their number. Amongst them were five Irish soldiers, from various regiments, who all died.[210]

The largest regimental contingent in Number 2 hold came from the 1st Battalion Middlesex Regiment. There were numerous Irishmen amongst the Middlesex Regiment casualties. They died trapped in the holds when the ship sank, or were deliberately drowned by the Japanese afterwards.[211]

Initially, when the torpedoes exploded, the men in No. 2 hold took matters prosaically and even made jokes about their situation. But as the day wore on even these tough infantrymen started to show their fear. Their thirst worsened in the fetid heat, and they appealed, repeatedly, for water. Eventually the Japanese passed down two buckets of soiled, almost undrinkable, water – a lethally inadequate amount for over 1,100 men.

Conditions below became unbearable due to the lack of any toilet facilities. The Japanese response to this was as derisory as their response to the plea for drinking water. They passed down two old petrol tins to serve the toilet needs of hundreds of men. These desperately incontinent men passing foul-smelling diarrhoea, inside a dark unventilated steel box, caused an indescribable stench. However, the effects were far worse than merely being unpleasant. Nearly 200 of the men were suffering from diphtheria and the holds were a perfect breeding ground for cross-infection. And many men who survived the sinking died subsequently from infections, probably caught whilst in the hold.

Around 7.30 p.m., the Japanese troops were taken off by another ship. Then the small hatches above the British troops were covered with tarpaulins and battened down, leaving the men trapped inside in total darkness.

In No. 3 hold, the weakened emaciated soldiers had a task that would have defeated men in the peak of health. They were manning hand-operated pumps, thrown down by the Japanese, in a losing battle to try to pump out the seawater that was slowly rising up inside the ship. The hold contained around 380 gunners from the Royal Artillery. There were many Irishmen amongst them; they all died.[212] The gunners laboured on the pumps in relays through the night. Every few minutes the men pumping collapsed, then the next batch took over until they too collapsed from exhaustion and lack of oxygen.

By the following morning it was clear to everyone onboard that the Japanese intended to kill them by leaving them locked inside the ship as it sank. All the Japanese military passengers and crew had been evacuated. A six-man suicide squad had been left onboard to stop the POWs escaping through the hatches. And half a dozen Japanese ships were lying nearby not to rescue them, but for a far more sinister purpose.

At around 8.30 a.m., over twenty-four hours since the first torpedo had struck, the ship gave another lurch. Colonel Stewart gave the order to break out of the hold. Using a butcher's knife, that someone had hidden away, they cut open some of the lashings on the hold coverings, pushed some planks aside and started scrambling through the hatch. The Japanese soldiers immediately started shooting the men as they came out on deck.

There was a brief moment of panic in No. 2 hold, as hundreds of desperate men jostled to get onto the two flimsy wooden ladders leading up to the hatch. This is the point at which leadership and British Army regimental tradition prevented a total disaster. Colonel Stewart was deeply respected by the men in his regiment. When he spoke men listened. Colonel Stewart called out, 'Steady – Steady the Middlesex [Regiment], remember who you are.'[213] Order was quickly restored and the men formed disciplined queues for the ladders enabling most of them to get on deck.

The six Japanese guards kept shooting prisoners as they climbed out the hatch. But there were so many that they just couldn't shoot them all. Some of the POWs ran across to holds No. 1 and No. 3 and loosened the hatch covers. In No. 1 hold men waiting on the steps underneath forced off the wooden hatch-boards and then rushed out on deck.

By now rifle fire was coming from the half dozen Japanese boats that had been waiting nearby, and men started to jump into the water. At No. 3 hold, nineteen-year-old Gunner Jack Etiemble desperately waited for someone to undo the hatches and let them out. The soldier on deck doing this loosened the cover but was shot by one of the Japanese suicide squad. Etiemble: 'We managed to loosen a few more [planks] and started climbing out. The Japs were still shooting from the patrol boats. I managed to get out and was lying on deck waiting for a break in the shooting, before sliding into the water.'[214]

Many of the gunners escaped and some of them overpowered the Japanese suicide squad. Then the wooden ladder broke trapping the remainder of the gunners in No. 3 hold. Etiemble:

Just after the escape ladder gave way ... I heard an Irish gunner shout 'we cannot get out, let's give them a song'. They sang 'It's a long way to Tipperary'. I slid down into the water, knowing the Gunners had done their duty in spite of the adverse conditions. No water, no food, no air. They had kept the ship afloat for twenty-four hours, and no one need have died ...[215]

On deck medical teams tried to get the worst of the casualties onto makeshift rafts. Lance Corporal Egan, from Dublin, recalled that Colonel Stewart, 'worked amongst the sick and wounded onboard and carried men to rafts'.[216] Other men went back down into Nos 1 and 2 holds to evacuate the POWs still trapped there. Warrant Officer Evans:

> [Then] suddenly the ship sank entirely, the bows going underneath in something less than a minute when she gave her final lurch and disappeared under the sea entirely … more hundreds of men were thrown into the sea and all who were able made their way by swimming or raft towards the auxiliary craft in the hope of being picked up.[217]

Sapper Taylor (Royal Engineers) swam around like the rest, looking for help:

> There were 5 Japanese naval craft sailing around the boat, but were not at first picking up any of the POWs. I observed on one occasion where a rope was thrown over the side, a man climbed up and as he reached the top of the rope, a member of the crew took out his revolver and shot point blank at the man who fell back into the water.[218]

This scenario was repeated dozens of times as men swam towards what should have been rescue. Instead they found themselves being shot at or lured into climbing ropes up the side of a boat to be met with a bayonet thrust. Many soldiers, seeing what was happening, started to swim towards some distant islands.

When the first British soldiers scrambled ashore, the Chinese realised who they were. They had previously assumed it was Japanese soldiers in the water. This part of China was under Japanese military occupation and millions of Chinese civilians had been murdered during the last decade. The Chinese hadn't been interested in going out to help what they thought were

Japanese troops, but now boats, manned by fishermen, sailed out and started rescuing men from the water. This is probably what influenced the Japanese to stop murdering the survivors, since it became clear that there would be too many witnesses.

A Japanese boat picked up a group of sick and wounded men that Surgeon Lieutenant Jackson (Limerick), and other medical staff, had tried to keep floating together. Jackson operated on one man as they headed ashore: 'Able Seaman Thomas Eccleston had a wounded leg that had turned gangrenous. He [Jackson] operated [on Eccleston] on the boat as it cut through the surf, with only a blunt razor blade as an instrument; Eccleston lived.'[219]

Strong tides and currents continued to take a toll as weakened men slid beneath the waves. Eventually more swimmers and men clinging on to makeshift rafts and debris began to wash ashore on the nearest islands. Gunner Michael Maher, from Dublin: 'Accompanied by Lance Bombardier Denton, [we] swam to a small island – [we] hid for two days but was found by Nip [Japanese] Marines.'[220]

The local Chinese were desperately poor. But they fed and clothed the hundreds of men despite the risk to themselves, as the Japanese were likely to kill them if found helping POWs. Eventually, Japanese soldiers visited each island searching for the POWs. Some men tried to hide. Three Royal Navy Warrant Officers, Fallace, Evans and Johnstone, who spoke Chinese, persuaded the fishermen to help them escape. The three men hid amongst rocks along the sea shore. A few days later, after the Japanese had given up searching, they were taken by Chinese resistance fighters to the mainland and smuggled out of occupied China to the British Embassy at Chungking.

Aside from these three, the 1,006 men who'd survived the sinking were recaptured and taken to Shanghai. A few were so desperately sick that the Japanese decided to leave them there. But the bulk of the *Lisbon Maru* survivors were put onboard another Hellship, the *Washington Maru*, and sent to Osaka in Japan.

The Japanese government tried to use the sinking of the *Lisbon Maru* as a propaganda opportunity. George Hamilton, an officer in the Royal Scots, recalled:

> Shortly after we arrived in Osaka some of us were informed that we would be permitted to broadcast messages to our families, and that we could include information about how the 'wicked' Americans had sunk the 'unarmed' POW ship and how grateful we were to the 'gallant' Nipponese for saving our lives.[221]

This was a lie, though it must have been a tempting proposition as everyone was keen to reassure their families that they were alive. Nonetheless, they refused and were then told that broadcasts could be made containing personal messages only. This next offer was accepted by the senior British officers:

> After some anxious discussions about whether this would be contrary to King's Regulations we concluded that there could be no objection; and we informed the men that if there were any repercussions after the war we would inform the authorities that we had so advised them.[222]

On 18 November, just over two weeks after the *Lisbon Maru* sank, Japan made the first survivors' broadcast. It was not done for humanitarian reasons, it was an exercise in propaganda aimed at causing discord between the Allies. The Japanese Domei news agency had already put out a series of statements, including one, on 11 November, purporting to come from Lieutenant Colonel Stewart. They claimed that 'Stuart' said that, 'no words can express his chagrin over the fact that so many of his comrades are no longer with him because of the thoughtlessness and reckless conduct of an American submarine.'[223]

Colonel Stewart said absolutely no such thing. But effective propaganda campaigns use as much truth as possible to add a layer of authenticity to the intended message. This is why some POWs were allowed to send a message to their families. On 18 November, Japan broadcast a radio programme called the *British and Australian War Prisoners Hour*. The Japanese announcer began, in English, 'The first voice you hear will be that of J. Casey aged 42 of the Royal Navy, home address Union House, County Cork, Eire.'[224] Then Casey's recording was played:

> This is Stoker J. Casey of the Royal Navy speaking: Anyone hearing this message kindly convey it to Mrs Casey, Union House, County Cork, Eire. After being captured in Hong Kong we were kept nine months there, where we were treated well. We were removed on 27th September to Japan. The ship unfortunately met a submarine which caused a great loss of life among us. I was picked up by the Japanese Navy and fortunately arrived in Japan where I was treated very well.[225]

To the POWs the details were less important than letting their families know they were alive. The messages were picked up by the BBC Monitoring Service and the Red Cross informed Casey's family about the broadcast. A few days later, on 2 December, they received a letter from the Army with the same information.

Casey was very ill, as were many *Lisbon Maru* survivors and other POWs already in the Osaka region. Surgeon Lieutenant Jackson was tasked with establishing Ichioka POW hospital. Though the Japanese authorities intended it as a containment area rather than a facility to help the sick and wounded. The venue was under the stands at the Osaka Stadium. Despite a lack of drugs, Jackson, with the aid of some Royal Navy sick-berth artificers and other personnel, worked tirelessly for the POWs. Roly Dean, an Australian soldier (originally born in England), was sent there from the Kawasaki Shipyards. Dean described Ichioka as dark, dingy, and infested with body lice and bedbugs, a place where death was a frequent visitor.[226]

The patients were all on half rations. Despite this, morale at Ichioka was higher than might be expected. Dean put this down to the efforts of Doctor Jackson, who always found time to examine new patients and give them what help he could no matter how busy he was.[227]

Stoker Casey was also at Osaka Stadium with Surgeon Lieutenant Jackson. Casey: '[Jackson] performed magnificent acts of surgery despite rigid opposition from ignorant Jap medical [personnel] and he suffered punishment by the Japs because he fought for sick and dying prisoners.'[228]

Petty Officer Robert Hosford, from Dublin, also survived the *Lisbon Maru*. He'd served on HMS *Tamar*, in Hong Kong, with Petty Officer Casey. Both men, as members of *Tamar's* Petty Officers' mess, would have known each other socially as well as professionally. In happier times they would have enjoyed the odd drink together in the mess. Hosford's family, like many others, spent the war wondering if their loved one was alive or not. His sister: 'six months [after the surrender of Hong Kong] I heard he was a prisoner, and then nothing further until the Japanese reported him missing after the sinking of the *Lisbon Maru*.'[229]

About a month after the sinking, the interpreter Niimori, returned to Hong Kong. The POWs loathed him. He'd greeted them on the dockside in Shanghai with the words, 'none of you should be here, you were all meant to die like rats in a trap'.[230] Sometimes Niimori drunkenly boasted about closing down the hatches on the *Lisbon Maru*. But the *Lisbon Maru* massacre was so traumatic that even the perpetrators were affected.

Emily Hahn was one of the very few civilian internees repatriated from Hong Kong, before the end of the war, 'It had been a bad time for the women whose men had disappeared … and we talked about nothing else. [But the] one mitigating factor in the dreadful days after the sinking was that we believed Niimori too had been lost.'

Before Niimori sailed on the *Lisbon Maru* he'd been the most hated of the Japanese officers the female internees had to deal with. But:

> After he [Niimori] came back he was a changed man. He became sympathetic, helpful ... [and became] the most popular of the officers with whom we dealt. I have often wondered if the sinking of the *Lisbon Maru*, and the scenes he must have witnessed, didn't shock him into reform.[231]

But for most of the POWs nothing positive emerged from the *Lisbon Maru*. Many survivors never recovered from their experiences. Research, conducted post-war, revealed that one man was so traumatised that for two years he couldn't cope with living indoors and made a den for himself in his parent's garden shed. Others were unable to face seeing their families at all. Some committed suicide.[232]

20

JAPAN

The Japanese Army transported POWs from Hong Kong and Java to Japan, from as early as September 1942. In 1944 it was decided to increase the labour force in Japan by drawing on the newly enlarged pool of labour returned to Singapore and Java from the Burma Railway. Many of the men sent from Singapore were almost glad to go to Japan. They reasoned that nothing could be as bad as the Railway and that things could only get better. The POWs from Hong Kong could have told them differently …

The journey to Japan proved the undoing of many POWs whose weakened bodies succumbed to disease, heatstroke, suffocation, starvation, and myriad other causes, whilst packed into the holds of Hellships. Others drowned when ships, lacking the Red Cross markings that should have been displayed on POW transports, were sunk by American and British submarines. The remainder landed in Japan and quickly found that starvation and brutality remained the norm. And they suffered the shock in winter of exchanging tropical heat for sub-zero temperatures whilst being denied adequate clothing or footwear.

A measure of the POWs' desperation is that some of them even tried to escape from Japan. They were on an island, hundreds of miles from any hope of safety; immediately recognisable by their appearance, they had no chance of blending in amongst the civilian population and nowhere to hide. Lance Corporal Michael Walsh, from Skibbereen, was imprisoned at Kobe Camp. Walsh: 'Private Smith and Private Rodaway, 2nd [battalion] Loyal Regiment [escaped] in the spring of 1944.

[They were] recaptured two days later. They were paraded in view of the troops on the parade ground handcuffed to military police. They were not seen again.'[233]

The POWs worked in coal mines, copper mines, shipyards, quarries and factories. Many of these were owned by Japanese companies like Mitsubishi, Kawasaki and Toyota. These firms thrived on the influx of slave labour and eventually went on to become internationally successful. Years later, former (civilian and military) slave labourers demanded reparations for their work. The companies shirked their responsibilities, denied liability, and the claims were rejected by the Japanese courts. And the American and British governments, concerned with securing Japan as a Cold War ally, had little enthusiasm for helping to press claims.

Captain Michael Murphy, from Cork, became a POW slave labourer for the Mitsubishi Corporation, in Yokohama docks. In December 1942, after only a month in the shipyard, the consequences of working for Mitsubishi were made plain: He was one of the soldiers whose duty it was to wash the corpses of other POWs, wrap them in a blanket inside a wooden box, and then transport them to a crematorium three miles away. Amazing as it might sound, this was a duty that the POWs actually looked forward to, as the cremations were occasionally carried out with Buddhist rites, and the POWs who brought the coffin would be given a cup of tea and, possibly, a biscuit.

In camps outside of Japan, the Japanese authorities didn't care if dead POWs were buried or left to rot. Within Japan bodies were disposed of correctly, usually by cremation. Nonetheless, it might seem incredulous that men should look forward to carrying their friends' corpses away to be cremated. The psychological distancing that POWs had to acquire in the face of death enabled them to cope with *having* to do this. But it doesn't explain relishing the task: in this instance they enjoyed it because they were sometimes given a couple of cigarettes and some tea – a telling reflection of their nutritional state.

A few months later Captain Murphy met a fellow Irishman, Stoker Ashcroft from Carrigaline, Cork. Naturally they chatted and exchanged stories, and Ashcroft told Murphy about his experiences during the sinking of HMS *Repulse.*

Leading Stoker Ashcroft had been captured in the Banka Straits attempting to escape from Singapore. After being imprisoned at Palembang (Sumatra), Changi, and Formosa, he was sent out to Japan. He did all he could to hinder Mitsubishi's corporate success. Alshcroft: 'My work entailed caulking and riveting. Faulty work was passed unknown to the inspectors and whenever possible machinery was put out of commission by me.'[234]

Trooper Edward Ryan, from Limerick, was another of the Irish POWs taken from Java and Sumatra to Japan. He'd been imprisoned at Tandjong Priok (Java), where news of the sinking of the *Lisbon Maru* and the death of the POWs reached the men via a smuggled local newspaper. His feelings, contemplating his own imminent voyage, can only be imagined.

In Japan, the POWs were assigned to any one of a number of administrative districts. Ryan was sent to Fukuoka district, which contained numerous POW camps and work sites in southern Honshu and northern Kyushu. He arrived at Camp No. 8, Motoyama, near Shimonoseki, probably in or around November 1942. The men worked down a coal mine, in freezing cold weather, with little in the way of warm clothing. The normal POW ailments, like dysentery and vitamin deficiency diseases, took their toll. Constant throat and eye infections, caused by coal dust, and the danger of mine collapses added to their misery.

At Motoyama, as in other camps, the prisoners took what few pleasures they could when they could. Captain Duncan, a British officer, described hearing Trooper Ryan sing:

The Japs allow the men to hold sing-songs on Wed and Saturdays between 7pm and 9pm. And there is an Irishman

called Ryan in the billet [hut] next door to us who gives a
remarkably good imitation of a female voice; last night [10
March 1943], he suddenly started singing soprano and the
sentry who was walking up and down outside, stopped and
then darted into the billet to see who the female was!!!²³⁵

Another place in the Fukuoka administrative archipelago has
become known to us all – Nagasaki. There were a number
of POW camps nearby. Squadron Leader Aidan MacCarthy
(Cork) found himself acting as Senior British Officer at one,
after all Allied officers, except medical officers and padres,
were moved to Manchuria.

The senior officer (or NCO) in a POW camp was held
responsible for any problems with the POWs or the internal administration of the camp. If anything went wrong the
Japanese would punish him. The senior officer also had the
duty of representing the POWs, and interceding on their
behalf, regarding rations and treatment and so on. When a
senior officer did this conscientiously, he would invariably
suffer at the hands of the Japanese.

MacCarthy's camp worked for the Mitsubishi Corporation
shipyards, and then (in late 1944) a factory, in Nagasaki. After
nearly three years slaving for Mitsubishi, many of the POWs
were on the edge of death. When they were allowed to send
a Red Cross postcard home to their next of kin, it provided
a small, but valuable, boost to morale. But it had unexpected
consequences for the Irish POWs. MacCarthy:

There were twelve POWs in our camp with Southern
Irish addresses and, after the first batch of outgoing mail
had been sorted, we were summoned to the office of the
Commandant … We Irish had it seemed, joined forces with
the British to wage war against the Japanese people, who
were only defending themselves against the brutal attacks of
the American and Commonwealth warmongers. Because

of our bad actions we must be punished … [with] a beating
from the Commandant himself.[236]

In 1945 they were moved to an opencast coal mine about two
miles outside Nagasaki. MacCarthy continued in his role as
both Senior British Officer and camp doctor. The prisoners'
physical condition worsened and as more men died they were
placed in barrels and cremated. The start of American bombing raids over Nagasaki brought some cheer to the POWs as
did news of the defeat of Germany in May 1945. After this the
POWs under MacCarthy's command were forced to dig their
own mass grave. MacCarthy:

> [We had to dig] a pit about six foot deep and about twenty
> foot square. Whilst we were digging, civilian carpenters
> began to erect a long wooden platform about fifteen feet
> from the edge of the hole. The platform would be used to
> mount the machine guns which would carry out our slaugh-
> ter – as and when the authorities decided to eliminate us. We
> dug on incredulously, our feelings numbed. To dig one's own
> grave is an extraordinary sensation. A sense of *déjà-vu* seems
> almost to overtake one. I had a fantasy glimpse of my own
> shot-up corpse lying in the watery mud.[237]

In fact, similar measures took place at most POW camps. The
end of the war was in sight, and Japan expected an Allied invasion. According to an Australian POW, MacCarthy, aided by
Sergeant Major Des Mulcahy (Australian Army), they had pre-
pared a plan to break out to try and reach the coast.[238]

But on 6 August 1945 something happened that would
save the POWs' lives and, in the long term, change the world
we live in forever. An American B29 dropped an atomic
bomb on the Japanese city of Hiroshima. Sergeant Ernest
Williams, from Cork, Private Michael O'Connor, from
Ballybunnion, and Battery Quartermaster Sergeant Kenneth

Cluff, from Stradbally, were amongst the Irish soldiers who stood witness.

Three days later, on 9 August, Aidan MacCarthy watched as two B29 bombers heading north changed direction and flew towards Nagasaki. He ran to the air-raid shelter along with some men returned early from a working party. Two men didn't bother to go inside and stood looking up at the sky. MacCarthy:

> One of them shouted to us that three small parachutes had dropped. There then followed a blue flash, accompanied by a very bright magnesium-type flare which blinded them. Then came a frighteningly loud, but rather flat, explosion which was followed by a blast of hot air.[239]

They left the shelter to find a scene of chaos. Dead and mutilated bodies lay around. The wooden camp buildings had carbonised and fires, stoked up by exploding gas mains, burned out of control. Wounded people ran around with burnt skin and hands clasped over blinded eyes. In the distance, MacCarthy's gaze was met by a twisted forest of steel girders that was all that remained of concrete buildings:

> But most frightening of all was the lack of sunlight – in contrast to the bright August sunshine that we had left a few minutes earlier, there was now a kind of twilight. We all genuinely thought, for some time, that this was the end of the world.[240]

21

LIBERATION

When Japan surrendered to the Allies most men were too physically and mentally exhausted to do more than give silent thanks for their survival. Their immediate problem was to secure the handover of control of their camp from the Japanese and to maintain their own security whilst awaiting the arrival of Allied forces.

All of the POWs required ongoing medical care of some sort. Air drops of medicines, food, and clothing alleviated the situation to some extent. But some men, like Corporal Daniel Carroll RAF, from Kilkenny, died after the war ended whilst awaiting repatriation.

A few men took the opportunity to exact revenge on their former captors. A POW described to this author how he was encouraged, by a *very* senior officer, to deal with some of the worst of his former torturers: '[Name] gave us revolvers and we went to the hut where the nine Japs were. We kicked the door in and killed them all. We didn't bury the bodies, just left them there. I think there was a lot more of this sort of thing going on than people admit or realise.'[241]

This was, of course, illegal. Though, given the bestial treatment that the Far East POWs were subjected to, it's surprising that the urge to seek summary justice wasn't more widespread.

After the Japanese capitulation Squadron Leader MacCarthy took command of the camp where he'd been imprisoned: 'I placed our previous [Japanese] Commandant in a cell in the guardroom – more for his own safety than for anything else. He was now a very frightened man. He had every reason to be. A number of the POWs had been all set to hang him immediately.'[242]

MacCarthy's decision saved the Commandant's life, though two Australian soldiers still managed to break in and beat him up. Their anger and hatred was so strong that one of them, literally, bit the Commandant's ear off.

But most POWs were so ill that all their remaining energy was occupied in foraging for food and looking after their even sicker mates. When the first Allied troops reached the camps, and saw these men, it left a profound and lasting impression upon them. In Singapore, Des Francis, a Royal Marine serving onboard the British cruiser HMS *Sussex*, was one of the first men to see the POWs in Changi jail:

> We arrived in Singapore about three days after the surrender of Japan. On docking I began to hear rumours regarding the physical conditions of men from the liberated camps. I'd be lying if I were to say these comments unduly concerned me. I don't mean this in a callous way, but I'd served through an entire World War and all participants had seen death and slaughter on a huge scale. So in certain ways I felt impervious to human suffering.[243]

But the pitiful emaciated creatures in Changi shocked Francis to a degree that he would never have believed possible:

> The first thing that struck me when entering the camp [Changi] was the terrible smell. On attempting to recollect it words honestly fail me. It's been stated by other people who visited camps throughout the world that they could smell death in the air – I can't find more fitting words. The place was infested with all manner of insects and vermin and the poor souls who'd lived in this filth for the length of the war were [by now] totally oblivious to it.[244]

Even half a century later the sorrow and anger is clear when Francis recalls how he tried to talk to the POWs:

It was difficult to know what to say and I felt nervous when shaking their hands because they were all so frail I was truly scared of hurting them. After this night some of the lads began spending time on our ship, mainly just for a bite to eat or for a chat. In some ways I felt better when talking to them in a more relaxed atmosphere as I could see the Japs hadn't succeeded in breaking their spirits. Although for some it was sadly too late – they were so far gone from illness even our Medical Staff could not save them – they died whilst still within the confines of Singapore. I think this was the hardest thing of all to come to terms with, after years of untold misery when freedom finally beckoned death took them from us. It was so sad to watch. For myself I will never forgive the Japanese for what they did to these defenceless men.[245]

The liberation of the Hong Kong POWs was no less shocking. Army nurse Sister Irene Anderson served onboard the hospital ship SS *Tairea*. Over 500 civilian prisoners, many of them women and small children, were taken onboard. Anderson, despite being a qualified military nurse with war experience, was shocked by the condition of the women and children. She described the frightened and overwhelmed infants as little bits of bone held together by skin. Like many of the servicemen and women tasked with caring for children who had been incarcerated in the prison camps, she was filled with hatred for the Japanese.

One sight that especially moved her was watching an Irish woman – who had not been interned because of being a neutral – being reunited with her (British) husband and children. The Japanese Army had imprisoned her children, as they were considered to be British, and this was the first time she had seen them for three and a half years.[246]

22

POST WAR

The long-term effects of the Japanese slave-labour camps reached beyond the POWs to their families. Christopher Brooks, an English soldier in the Royal Artillery, died in 1942. He was drowned when the *Lisbon Maru* sank. His Irish wife was evacuated from Hong Kong before the final battle for the island. She spent the rest of the war struggling to bring up two small children alone. In January 1943 she was informed that Christopher Brooks was missing at sea. In August 1945 she received official confirmation that her husband had died three years earlier.

It's hard to imagine the strain and anxiety, the lonely hours clinging to hope, which must have filled those three years. Their son, Ron Brooks, has no doubt of the effects:

> The most important aspect to me is how my father's death and all the events of that time affected and shortened my mother's life. Looking back on my mother's background from provincial Cork, how she married a British soldier and was transported to the [then] relatively exotic locations of Malta and Hong Kong, makes the tragedy more poignant as her life all fell apart and she was left to cope with two young boys far from her home and family. She died from TB in 1949.[247]

As for the POWs themselves, many met an early death after the war from illnesses linked to their former captivity. Ill health dogged the remaining years of those who made it to old age. George Simmonds, a former FEPOW, described his return home:

We came home skin and bones – that's how it was. I recovered quite well. After I came home I had a dream night after night. I was still on [HMS] *Prince of Wales*. I was lying in my hammock and we were in a bombing [air] raid and the bombs were falling and they were going right through me and exploding somewhere underneath. And I wasn't hurt because I knew I wasn't there. But the dreams kept coming on and on and on, and it was some considerable time before that disappeared. So I think I was most probably a bit mad at that time.[248]

George clearly suffered from Post Traumatic Stress Disorder (PTSD). This was a common problem amongst former FEPOWs. George feels that he was lucky because he recovered. He was able to compartmentalise his experiences and leave them behind him: 'I got married, and ordinary life took over, children, a job. There was rationing still. We had more troubles than we wanted without thinking about what had happened. You were alive and that was it.'[249]

Many POWs were far less successful than George in dealing with the psychological aftermath of the camps. Simmonds: 'That was something that happened in our lives and now it's gone, [but] I've seen men that in my opinion, have ruined their lives by not being able to leave it behind. They've lived it day after day after day.'[250]

Most POWs remained embittered about the actions of their former captors. Dermot Cullen, from Dublin, served with the British Expeditionary Force in France, escaped at Dunkirk, and then was captured by the Japanese after being sent out to the Far East. His nephew remembers that, 'he never said anything bad about the Germans, despite his experiences at Dunkirk, but he remained very bitter about the Japanese.'[251]

For some Far East POWs the war never really finished. Others achieved limited degrees of closure aided by alcohol, medication, or counselling. Harold Lock recalled how

he coped, using alcohol, when he returned to his home in
Sudbury, Suffolk, in 1945:

> There were a few of us in Sudbury who'd been POWs in
> the Far East. We used to stay out all day and evening drink-
> ing, getting drunk. If we got into any minor bits of bother
> locally the police would generally turn a blind eye. People
> round here knew what we'd been through and they made
> allowances.[252]

Harold Lock spent three and a half years accumulated back pay
from the Royal Navy, a considerable sum of money, on alcohol. But it brought him through the immediate aftermath of
his experiences and he eventually settled down, married, and
lived a normal life. He worries, with some justification, that
the experiences of the POWs will soon be forgotten.

Gordon Smale found his salvation by remaining in the Royal
Navy after the war and volunteering for hazardous duties,
removing minefields in the Mediterranean. He even visited
Japan, something that many former POWs could never contemplate. After twenty-two years of distinguished service in
the Royal Navy he retired and put his energies towards home,
family, and a new civilian career. Like most survivors of the
Japanese POW camps, Gordon maintained an outward show of
composure and kept his inner torments to himself. As, indeed,
these men were encouraged to do when they first returned
home. Officially, they were advised not to talk about their experiences and to maintain a stiff upper lip and get on with life.

So in addition to the long-term effects of tropical diseases, veteran reality was a life of hidden emotional turmoil.
Occasional meetings with former POWs provided peer support from the only men who could truly understand how they
felt. Professional intervention came from organisations like
Combat Stress, a charity set up to care for men and women
psychologically traumatised by their experiences during war.

'I'm off to Twit House again', Gordon Smale would some-times declare (to the author). Twit House was his irreverent, but appreciative, nickname for Tyrwhitt House, a Combat Stress treatment centre that provides professional (and free) counselling for PTSD. Tyrwhitt House possibly kept Gordon Smale alive with the help they gave him. They have probably meant the difference between life and death for a great many British and Irish veterans.

There are others though who fall through the net and kill themselves. The link between wartime traumatic experi-ence and suicide is now well known. In 1982, following the Argentine invasion and occupation of the Falkland Islands, 253 British servicemen died fighting in the Falklands War. And since then more Falkland's veterans have committed suicide than were killed during the war. At least 148 Irish POWs died in the camps, between 1942 and 1945. How many Irish survi-vors, haunted by flashbacks, and worn down reliving the past in recurring nightmares, killed themselves? We will never know …

The fact that a hugely disproportionate percentage of vet-erans sleep rough on Britain's streets or are incarcerated in prison is now well known, albeit less well cared about. Experts argue over exact figures, but perhaps 15 per cent of current rough sleepers are veterans of the armed services. So, during the 1950s and '60s, how many former British and Irish POWs slept rough, stared at by contemptuous passers-by, unaware of their past? Again, we will never know.

In 1951 the Japanese government awarded British POWs (including Irishmen who served in Britain's armed forces) the insultingly low sum of £76 each in compensation. Former civilian internees were awarded an even more derisory £49. Japan was not the immensely wealthy nation it is today, and it was claimed that these sums were all that could be afforded.

In the following years survivors tried hard to forget the past but eventually they decided to seek justice. Veterans' organisa-tions struggled through the Japanese court system seeking a realistic level of compensation for former POWs. Then a visit to the United Kingdom by the Japanese Emperor proved a focus for demands from veterans for both a formal apology from Japan and adequate compensation. In a speech at the Guildhall, London, in 1998, the Emperor made a comment, about his country's 'deep sorrow and pain' for the suffering inflicted during the Second World War. Many former POWs felt this fell far short of anything like a meaningful apology.

The veterans appealed to the British Prime Minister Tony Blair for support. Predictably, the interests of international trade, and big business, took precedence over war veterans. Finally, in 2000, the British government brought in its own scheme. This allowed FEPOWs to make a claim for an ex-gratia payment of £10,000.

The surviving POWs finally received some compensation. Though do they ever make wry comparisons and wonder quite where society's values lie. Far East POWs experienced three and a half years of labour, starvation, torture, and disease, leading to severe physical and psychological trauma; for this they received £76 from the Japanese government and £10,000 from the British government. For burning herself with the hot coffee she bought from McDonalds, a lady in the USA received £2,000,000.[253]

23

HOW AND WHY?

How did anyone survive incarceration in a Japanese POW camp? Luck, fortune, call it what you will, played some part in this survival lottery. Men who remained in Changi camp throughout captivity were far more likely to survive than those sent to the Railway. Officers received more pay than enlisted men and therefore had a slightly better chance of survival because they could afford to buy a little more food from the Japanese. A few men were sent to a show camp in Indochina, maintained in reasonable condition by the Japanese, in order to hoodwink the International Red Cross: Most men sent to this camp survived the war. Yet others, who were sent to Sandakan, though they didn't know it when they went, received a death sentence.

Whilst the POWs had no say over where they were sent, they had a choice in their response to captivity. Some men, ground down by incessant labour, starvation, disease, and violence, gave up the struggle, seeing death as a merciful release from their misery. And those of us fortunate enough never to have been tested by such horrors should not criticise them.

So some men stopped trying to live, whilst others died of diseases so bad that attitude or philosophy was irrelevant. But as one former POW said, 'there was something those of us who survived had in common, and that was that we had the *will* to survive.'[254] Another former POW made the point plain with an example. George Simmonds:

We were in one camp – we had men from 134 Field Regiment, Royal Artillery, they were a Territorial unit from Blackpool. One of the chaps, Ernie Lee, he was two penn'orth of skin and bone to start with [before being imprisoned]. He went into the hospital hut with dysentery, and whatever else that was going Ernie had got it. Day after day when we came in from work they said 'see [visit] Ernie, most probably you'll have to bury him tomorrow'. But he survived and came home, whilst there were big fit [pre-war] men that had a touch of malaria to begin with and they just died. It doesn't really make sense, but we saw it happen. Those that you expected to bury because they were in a very poor way somehow hung on. And what you'd call big strong men, the slightest illness, though none of them were really slight, they just died.[255]

On rare occasions men were so desperate to live that they collaborated with the Japanese. Either they informed on their fellow prisoners, or they voluntarily helped the Japanese camp administration. After the war an officer and some NCOs at Shamshuipo (Hong Kong) were subjected to disciplinary action for this.

Most British officers in Hong Kong, men like Colonel Stewart, co-operated only to the extent that they were forced to. So the Japanese selected someone more amenable. And Major Boon ran Shamshuipo POW camp, aided by a few men also willing to trade their honour for extra rations, in enthusiastic agreement with the wishes of the Japanese. Boon was also accused of revealing details of Allied escape plans to the Japanese. Private John Cawley, an RAMC medical orderly, from Ballymote, was one of the men who complained about the alleged traitorous actions by Major Boon: 'Some of the [escape] attempts were foiled by information given to the Japanese by Major Boon, British Camp Leader, and his subordinates. I suggest the fullest questioning of [the] men on the spot.'[256]

Boon was hated by POWs of all ranks. Soon after the Japanese surrender in 1945 Boon was arrested by another

POW Major Ryan, from Dublin. Boon was court-martialled in London in 1946 on charges of having voluntarily aided the Japanese while a prisoner of war at Shamshuipo Camp. However, the case against him wasn't proven and he was acquitted.

Anyone who aided the Japanese might gain extra rations or privileges from the Japanese. However, they also put themselves at serious risk from the anger of other POWs. A Sikh guard at Changi Camp, one of the Indian Army soldiers who deserted and served the Japanese as prison camp guards, was killed by the POWs. He used his bayonet on British prisoners once too often and was ambushed, and lowered, slowly, head first into a latrine and drowned.[257]

POWs did not forgive open collaboration with the enemy. A former POW recalled: 'We killed a number of our own men [during the war] for being Jap Happy. One day [name withheld] appeared dressed in Jap uniform. I asked him what the hell was going on – he said he just wanted to survive – men were getting desperate.'[258]

Why did the Japanese Army behave as it did? Adherence to the Geneva Conventions, to which Japan was signatory, should have ensured decent treatment for POWs. The conventions covered the types of work that POWs could do, their pay, food, living conditions, and the punishments they might be subjected to. Japan had signed and ratified the Hague Conventions of 1907. In 1929 the Japanese government signed the Geneva Conventions, which also included agreements regarding the treatment of POWs. But due to opposition from within the Japanese military the convention was never ratified.

Following the commencement of hostilities by Japan, the Allied nations sought a commitment from Japan that it would honour the terms of the convention. Japan promised that it would, so far as it was possible. Yet in practice the Japanese government failed to honour virtually any aspect of the convention.

This duplicity was not confined to the government. Repeatedly, when negotiating terms with Allied forces, local Japanese commanders agreed to honour the terms of the Geneva Conventions and subsequently reneged on their promise. Lieutenant Colonel Dobbin, from Cork, was serving as General Staff Officer to Major General Sitwell, who commanded the British troops in Java. Sitwell was responsible for negotiating the British, Australian, and American terms of surrender, following the decision of the Dutch government to cease fighting. Dobbin, as his GSO1, was intimately involved in the proceedings.

On 10 March the Air Officer Commanding (AOC) opened initial negotiations with Lieutenant General Maruyama, commanding the 2nd Japanese Guards Division. The following day the AOC, Sitwell, Brigadier Blackburn (Australian), and Colonel Searle (American), were summoned to Garoet. Sitwell:

> We spent the night at Bandoeng in chairs in a waiting room, and in the morning we assembled for the formal signing of the surrender terms … Maruyama promised, in front of numerous British and Japanese witnesses, that prisoners would be treated in all respects in accordance with the terms of the Geneva Convention, 1929. We were also ordered in future to obey all orders that might be given to us by any Japanese military officers. An attempt by the AOC to get the word 'lawful' inserted before 'orders' was refused point blank by Lt General Maruyama who stated that this was unnecessary since we had the protection of the Geneva Convention, under which no unlawful orders could be given to us.[259]

When Sitwell's negotiating officers returned to their own troops they warned them not to give away military information when questioned. On the basis of the promises just obtained, the troops were assured that they were protected from harm under the Geneva Conventions. The Japanese Army immediately made a mockery of this by torturing and executing a number of Allied officers for not revealing military information.

Bushido, the code of the Japanese warrior, is usually blamed for the torture and mistreatment of Allied POWs during the Second World War. However, Japan held German POWs captive during the First World War and their treatment was so impeccably civilised that many stayed on in Japan after the war, and their descendents live there to this day. At that time Japan was keen to absorb western, liberal, democratic ideals, and join the great powers at the high table. After the First World War, disappointed at perceived racial slights and ingratitude on the part of the Western powers, Japan reversed course and rejected Western values.

The route that took the Japanese Army from morality to the mass perpetration of rape, murder, and torture, is a complex one.[260] In the late nineteenth century Japan adopted Shinto as the State religion and decreed that the emperor should be worshipped as a living god. Commands given in the name of Emperor Hirohito, whether during the war in China, or in the prison camps of South East Asia, were the word of God: A situation that did not lend itself to the questioning of orders, neither from the POWs or their Japanese and Korean guards.

In the decade prior to the Japanese invasions in South East Asia, and the subsequent capture of thousands of Allied servicemen and women, the Japanese Army had been engaged in a war of conquest in Manchuria (China). The massive expansion in the size of the Japanese Army that this required came at the same time as a growing nationalist and militarist spirit took over Japanese political and social culture.

The expanded Japanese Army trained recruits by a methodology based on fear and brutality. Any mistake, no matter how minor, was punished by beatings with a fist or a bamboo stick. Officers beat NCOs, NCOs beat privates, privates beat senior recruits, and senior recruits beat junior recruits. It was a system based on blind unquestioning obedience and terror. And given that this was the norm within the Japanese Army, it was inevitable that similar disciplinary codes should have been imposed on its prisoners. Japanese soldiers were also taught that surrender was dishonourable. They were told that the spirit of Bushido demanded that they should kill themselves sooner than fall into the hands of the enemy. Hence the utter contempt felt by Japanese soldiers towards surrendered Allied servicemen.

Individually, Japanese soldiers were conditioned to believe that other races were inferior, and that some races, especially Chinese, were less than human. This was a concept that would later have lethal repercussions for the POWs. Within China, Japanese Army training methods employed levels of barbaric realism that seem hardly credible viewed in retrospect. Soldiers were blooded (taught to kill) by tying up and bayoneting Chinese civilians during mass executions. And rape, followed by the victim's murder, was encouraged as an individual and group activity.

Institutionally, the Japanese Army blooded itself in a series of campaigns against the Chinese Army and in numerous large-scale civilian massacres. Chinese sources estimate that 35 million Chinese military and civilian deaths occurred, during the Imperial Japanese Army's occupation of China, between 1931 and 1945.[261] In perhaps the most infamous massacre, which occurred in Nanking, in December 1937, the Japanese Army committed a series of atrocities over a period of six weeks, which resulted in the death of 300,000 people (about half of the city's population).

So Japanese soldiers were conditioned to kill without mercy, and brainwashed to think all other races were inferior or even sub-human. They were taught that it was a crime to surrender and that prisoners had no rights at all – not even the right to live. This was the army charged with the task of imprisoning captured Allied servicemen, in 1942.

24

FINALLY

The Emperor's Irish slaves endured a captivity of unremitting misery and pain. At times, researching this has been a saddening experience. One day in particular stands out. I was sitting in the National Archives at Kew, leafing through folders of wartime documentation. There was a packet wrapped in greaseproof paper tucked into the corner of one file. Curious, I opened it up and found a little pile of hand written Death Certificates. It was easy to see how they had been made. Sheets of Japanese scrap paper, about A4 size, had been torn across into strips. On one side of each strip was Japanese print. On the other side, neatly written in pencil, was the fading record of the death of a British Prisoner of War.

Each desperate little scrap of paper had the name, rank, number, and cause of death. Dysentery accounted for the demise of many of these, mostly, young men. The certificates in my hand reeked of torment and death. I could see, all too vividly, the long bamboo hut, and the rows of lice-ridden dying men tormented by mosquitoes, tropical heat and humidity. The doctor's anguish, his feelings of frustration, as he wrote each certificate knowing that his patients were dying from treatable diseases, felt palpably real. I was there and I could see it, feel it, and smell it. Overcome, I placed the Death Certificates back in their paper, as neatly folded as before, and walked outside to stand in the sunshine …

But the actions of the POWs themselves remain a source of inspiration. The courage and self sacrifice of the medical personnel stand out. The comradeship that could see a starving man give his own tiny ration of food to his mate, in an attempt to sustain his life for another day, is equally inspiring.

John Wyatt, a soldier from London, bedded down in a bamboo prison hut in Ban Pong (Thailand). The man next to him, Michael Shiels, from Dublin, was shivering and shaking, semi-conscious, with a bad bout of malaria. Wyatt found a piece of sacking, wrapped it around him, and then lay down beside him. The two men remained friends throughout their captivity, sharing scraps of food, caring for each other when they were ill. Wyatt: 'It's strange how fate throws people together. But [Mick Shiels] was to become my best mate until the end of our captivity and also back home in the UK.'[262]

Wyatt attended Shiels' wedding in Dublin after the war, and the two men remained close friends. When Michael Shiels eventually died, Wyatt, distraught with grief, described it as, 'the worst day of his life'.

Yes, researching the story of the Far East Prisoners of War was saddening. But it was also inspirational and uplifting. The POWs experienced the best and the worst – the courage and the depravity – that mankind is capable of. We would be foolish to forget such hard won lessons.

NOTES

1. Patrick Harrington, 1945.

2. *ibid*.

3. The term 'Jap Happy' was also used to refer to POWs who were perceived to be co-operating unnecessarily with the Japanese.

4. See R. Beattie, *The Death Railway* (TBRC Co. Ltd, 2009) for a full account.

5. F.G. Freeman, RAFVR in *Prisoners in Java* (Hamwic, 2007).

6. John Cawley, 1945, PRO Kew.

7. Sometimes confused with another composite battalion, the British Sumatra Battalion.

8. Bandsman Frederick Austin gives a full account of these events in the BBC Second World War People's War website.

9. Philip Clancy, 1945, PRO Kew.

10. *ibid*.

11. Russell Braddon, *The Naked Island* (Birlinn, 2005).

12. Philip Clancy, 1945, PRO Kew.

13. Jockie Bell, *Argyle and Sutherland Highlanders*. Quoted in Moffatt & Holmes McCormick, *Moon Over Malaya* (Tempus, 2002).

14. *ibid*.

15. M. Tsuji, *Japan's Greatest Victory* (Spellmount, 1997).

16. Gordon Smale. Interview with the author.

17. George Simmonds. Interview with the author.

18. The two capital ships carried, in total, 2,921 men, of whom 840 died.

19. George Simmonds. Interview with the author.

20. Gordon Smale. Interview with the author. The incident referred to is mentioned briefly in one or two books, and in some surviving documentation at the PRO. The account recorded by the officer and the account told to this author, not surprisingly, differ dramatically. This author firmly believes that Stoker Smale's account is the correct version of events. However, it falls outside of the scope of this book so is not discussed in detail.

21. Gordon Smale. Interview with the author.

22. Gunner Thomas Walsh, 1945, PRO Kew.

23. Captain James Gordon, 1945, PRO Kew.

24. Michael Hunt, 1945, PRO Kew.

25. *ibid*.

26. Captain James Gordon, 1945, PRO Kew.

27. E. Burgoyne, *Tattered Remnants* (Book Guild, 2002).

28. *ibid.*

29. Gordon Smale. Interview with the author.

30. *ibid.*

31. L. Gibson, *A Wearside Lad in World War II* (History of Education Project, 2005).

32. Sergeant (Pilot) Peter Ryan RAF, 1945, PRO Kew.

33. *ibid.*

34. *ibid.*

35. *ibid.*

36. Wing Commander Maguire, 1945, PRO Kew.

37. Letter from the Air Council to Mrs H.J. Maguire, 6 May 1942. Private Papers, IWM.

38. Postcard *c.* 1942-45. Air Marshall H.J. Maguire. Private Papers, IWM.

39. A. MacCarthy, *A Doctor's War* (Grubb Street, 2006).

40. Flying Officer Sid Scales in *Prisoners in Java* (Hamwic, 2007).

41. Squadron Leader Alan Giles RAF, 1945, PRO Kew.

42. *ibid.*

43. A. MacCarthy, *A Doctor's War* (Grubb Street, 2006).

44. Squadron Leader Alan Giles RAF, 1945, PRO Kew.

45. Flying Officer Sid Scales in *Prisoners in Java* (Hamwic, 2007).

46. Airman Alan Munro in *Prisoners in Java* (Hamwic, 2007).

47. Squadron Leader Alan Giles RAF, 1945, PRO Kew.

48. Squadron Leader Alan Giles RAF; Quoted on 100 Squadron Association website.

49. Edwin Loughlin, 4/19th Hyderabad Regiment. Letter to Sergeant Connolly's sister, December 1945.

50. *ibid.*

51. The basic chronology is taken from A/B Kenneally's own post-war written account. However, there is a possibility that he may not have recorded one link in the chain, a transfer via the German ship *Dresden*, before being moved to the *Ramses*.

52. Some accounts of the sinking of the *British Chivalry* give Captain Hill's birthplace as Belfast. His Japanese POW index card states both his place of birth and wife's address as Dublin.

53. BQMS Kenneth Cluff, 1945, PRO Kew.

54. *ibid.*

55. Patrick Moran, Francis Cullen, William Roe, Christopher Dodgson, James Monks, William Miller, Patrick Frain, John Hennessy.

56. Corporal Pease. IWM.

57. Corporal Patrick Crosbie, 1945, PRO Kew.

58. Massacre at the (Alexandra Road) British Military Hospital: eyewitness accounts. IWM.

59. Widders, R., *Spitting On A Soldier's Grave* (Matador, 2010).

60. Sergeant Cunliffe, 18th Battalion Reconnaissance Regiment. Statement made in 1942, PRO Kew. (Cunliffe escaped from Singapore.)

61. *ibid*.

62. M. Tsuji, *Japan's Greatest Victory*, (Spellmount Ltd, 1997).

63. Sergeant Cunliffe, 18th Battalion Reconnaissance Regiment. Statement made in 1942, PRO Kew.

64. Wilfred Theakstone, 1945, PRO Kew.

65. A. Cramsie, *Guest of an Emperor* (Family Edition, 1987).

66. Captain Brian Mayne, 1945, PRO Kew.

67. Major Gillachrist Campbell, 1945, PRO Kew.

68. *ibid*

69. The GOC (General Officer Commanding) at Singapore was General Percival. But at this stage he had been sent to Japan along with all other senior officers above the rank of Lieutant Colonel. Presumably Magill is referring to Lieutenant Colonel Holmes who took over command at Changi.

70. W.M. Magill, unpublished diary, 1942. IWM

71. *ibid*.

72. Sergeant Dermot O'Connor, 1945, PRO Kew.

73. Major Ernest Fillmore MBE, 1945, PRO Kew.

74. J.A. Richardson, *The War in Malaya – Diary*. TBRC.

75. *ibid*.

76. This is either Noel or Fergus Kennedy. Both men served in the Federated Malay States Volunteer Force.

77. L. West, *From Darjeeling to Down Under* (2004).

78. Lord Russell of Liverpool, *The Knights of Bushido* (Corgi 1960).

79. Former POW who was imprisoned in Java. Conversation with the author.

80. La Forte & Marcello (Ed.), *Building the Death Railway* (Scholarly Resources 1993).

81. Maurice O'Connell, interview with the author.

82. Report by Wing Commander Atkins, 1945, PRO Kew.

83. *ibid*.

84. *ibid*.

85. R. Pool, *Course For Disaster* (Leo Cooper, 1987).

86. Report by Lieutenant Stonor, 1945, PRO Kew.

87. Report by Wing Commander Atkins, 1945, PRO Kew.

88. *ibid*.

89. Mary Cooper came from Carrickmacross, County Monaghan. For both Edith Pedlow and Ruth Dickson, the Army Roll of Honour gives their place of origin as 'Eire'. Charlotte Black, Irene Wright and Edith Carroll came from Northern Ireland.

90. Spellings vary and it is sometimes referred to as Pompong, Pam Pong etc.

91. Sister Margot Turner, quoted in J. Smyth, *The Will To Live* (Cassell: London, 1970).

92. *ibid*.

93. *ibid*.

94. T. McGahan, Private Papers, 1985. IWM.

95. Sister Margot Turner, quoted in J. Smyth, *The Will To Live* (Cassell: London, 1970).

96. *ibid.*
97. *ibid.*
98. *ibid.*
99. *ibid.*
100. POWs and internees were forbidden, upon pain of death, to keep diaries and denied calendars and watches and so on. Chronological discrepancies between various accounts of the same event are common – and understandable.
101. B. Jeffrey, *White Coolies* (Angus and Robertson, 1954).
102. *ibid.*
103. *ibid.*
104. The events at Rabaul were described by one of the eighteen survivors, Gunner Alf Baker, in his memoir, *What Price Bushido*, published 1991.
105. The dates given on the Army Roll of Honour indicate that it was Hodson who died first, followed by Mallett and O'Connor. In this instance I have followed the narrative described by Gunner Alf Baker, who was one of the eighteen survivors.
106. L/Bdr Joseph Barrett, and Gunner John Bryant, from Dublin; Gunner Peter Keyes, Stradbally; Gunner James Moran, County Mayo; Bombardier William Perrott, Askeaton; Gunner Michael Walsh, County Wexford; Captain Henry Halsted, whose wife came from Waterford.
107. The Ballalle Island massacre is described in *Kill the Prisoners*, by Don Wall (1997).
108. Quoted in *Kill the Prisoners*, by Don Wall, (1997). The author was a FEPOW who worked on the Burma Railway,
109. *ibid.*
110. *ibid.*
111. Document No. 2710, certified as Exhibit 'O' in Doc. No.2687. NARA, RG 238 Box 2015. A copy of the original document can be seen courtesy of the Roger Mansell Centre For Research (Allied POWs Under the Japanese).
112. Gordon Smale, conversation with the author.
113. E. Gordon, *Through the Valley of the Kwai* (Wm Collins).
114. Private William Carleton, 1945, PRO Kew.
115. *ibid.*
116. *ibid.*
117. *ibid.*
118. WOII Ivor Williams, Royal Artillery, 1945, PRO Kew.
119. Private James Griffin, East Surrey Regiment, 1945, PRO Kew.
120. Sergeant John Hazard, Royal Corps of Signals, 1945, PRO Kew.
121. *ibid.*
122. G.S. Mowat, *The Rainbow through the Rain* (New Cherwell Press, 1995).
123. Paul Gibbs Pancheri, Volunteer, 1995.
124. A. Allbury, *Bamboo and Bushido* (Robert Hale Ltd, 1955).
125. *ibid.*
126. *ibid.*
127. Reay and Kenneally were serving with the 9th Battalion, Northumberland Fusiliers. Fitzgerald was serving on attachment to the Fusiliers, and Kelly was in the Royal Army Medical Corps.

128. Corporal Thomas Finn, 1st Battalion Manchester Regt, 1945, PRO Kew.

129. *ibid*.

130. *ibid*.

131. Lieutenant Colonel Dunlop, *War Diaries Of* (Penguin, 1986).

132. War Crimes Opening Address, TBRC.

133. Lieutenant Colonel Outram, 1945, TBRC.

134. PRO, Kew.

135. PRO, Kew.

136. Sergeant George Priestman, Sworn Affidavit, 1946, TBRC.

137. *ibid*.

138. Y. Tanaka, *Hidden Horrors* (Westview Press, 1996).

139. *ibid*.

140. Sergeant Peter Horan, RASC, 1945, PRO Kew.

141. He may possibly be referring to return springs.

142. Gunner Christopher Alston, 9 Coast Regiment RA, 1945, PRO Kew.

143. Gunner William Barter, 9 Coast Regiment RA, 1945, PRO Kew.

144. Gunner Michael Lynch, 88 Field Regiment RA, 1945, PRO Kew.

145. Gunner William Ivory, 5 Field Regiment RA, 1945, PRO Kew.

146. John Kenneally, 1945, PRO Kew.

147. Private Thomas McGrath, The Loyal Regiment, 1945, PRO Kew.

148. *ibid*.

149. Sergeant John Caddy, FMSVF, 1945, PRO Kew.

150. Sergeant Vincent Slavin, Royal Signals, 1945, PRO Kew.

151. Commander Vincent Walsh RN, 1945, PRO Kew.

152. *ibid*.

153. (Dr) R. Hardie, *The Burma-Siam Railway* (Imperial War Museum, 1983).

154. A. MacCarthy, *A Doctor's War* (Grubb Street, 2006).

155. *ibid*.

156. *ibid*.

157. *ibid*.

158. A. MacCarthy, *A Doctor's War* (Grubb Street, 2006).

159. Sapper Edward Brehony, Royal Engineers, 1945, PRO Kew.

160. Lance Sergeant Tomas Smith, 2nd AA Regiment, HKSRA, 1945, PRO Kew.

161. Captain Alfred Olson RAOC, 1945, PRO Kew.

162 Sworn Statement by Flight Lieutenant Parke, taken 5 September 1945, at Changi Jail.

163. Statistics courtesy of Rod Beattie, Thailand Burma Railway Centre.

164. J. Bradley, *Towards the Setting Sun* (JML Fuller, 1982).

165. D. Colonel, *War Diaries Of* (Penguin, 1986).

166. Private Patrick Carberry, RAOC, 1945, PRO Kew.

167. Interview with James Mudie given to Brian MacArthur, author of *Surviving the Sword* (Abacus, 2006).

168. Sergeant R. Thompson RAF in *Prisoners in Java* (Hamwic, 2007).

169. *ibid*.

170. Lieutenant Colonel Frederick McOstrich, 1945, PRO Kew.

171. Lance Corporal Philip Farrelly, 1945, PRO Kew.

172. Corporal Michael O'Donnell RAF, 1945, PRO Kew.
173. M. Ron & M. Johnathan *Baba Nonnie Goes To War* (Imprint, 2004).
174. Harold Lock. Interview with the author.
175. *ibid*.
176. *ibid*.
177. *ibid*.
178. Often spelled Haruku.
179. Harold Lock. Interview with the author.
180. *ibid*.
181. *ibid*.
182. Harold Lock. Interview with the author.
183. *ibid*.
184. Amongst them were Corporal Terrence Gleeson, LAC Francis Morgan, Sergeant William Tully and LAC Harold Williams. All four men came from Dublin and were in the RAF. Other Irishmen onboard the *Suez Maru* included Gunner Alex Morrow, from Drumbarron, and Flying Officer John Gregg, from Cork. Gregg, a former international athlete, was the son of the Primate of All Ireland.
185. Some sources dispute this and claim that one man survived and was picked up twenty-four hours later by an Australian corvette.
186. Lord Russell of Liverpool, *The Knights of Bushido* (Corgi, 1960).
187. John Wilson, Royal Corps of Signals, MI9 report, 1945, PRO Kew.
188. Captain John McQuillan RAMC, 1945 PRO Kew.
189. *ibid*.
190. Sergeant Michael Purcell, 3/6 Heavy AA Regt, RA., 1945, PRO Kew.
191. Annam was formerly a part of French Indochina - now part of Vietnam.
192. Sergeant Michael Purcell, 3/6 Heavy AA Regt, RA., 1945, PRO Kew.
193. Possibly (Purcell's) phonetic spelling.
194. Sergeant Michael Purcell, 3/6 Heavy AA Regt, RA., 1945, PRO Kew.
195. *ibid*.
196. Possibly a phonetic spelling.
197. Sergeant Michael Purcell, 3/6 Heavy AA Regt, RA., 1945, PRO Kew.
198. MI9, comments regarding Sergeant Michael Purcell, 1946, PRO Kew.
199. Mr Govier, quoted in Hong Kong War Diary website – Tony Banham.
200. The largest contingent served in the Middlesex Regiment: Lance Corporal John Burke, Cork; Privates Christopher Caul, Dublin; Michael Cullen, Dublin; Hugh Lynch, Cavan; Michael Ryan, Cork. Royal Artillery: Gunners Joseph Bell, Sligo; Ronald Weldrick, Dublin. Royal Engineers: Sappers Thomas Martin, Cobh; Richard Houston, Dublin; Edward Brennan, Dublin. RASC: Herbert Morgan. Royal Navy: Petty Officer Cornelius Cahalane, Skibbereen; Leading Stoker William Cooke, Roscommon.
201. Quoted in T. Banham, *The sinking of the Lisbon Maru* (HKUP, 2006); Diary, Blomfield, description of the arrival of prisoners from Hong Kong 15/9/42.
202. Edward Brennan, interrogation report, 1945, PRO Kew.
203. Anthony Eden, Statement to the House of Commons, 28/1/44.
204. Letter from the British Embassy, Chungking, to the Foreign Office;

29/12/42.

205. Lieutenant Howell, RASC, quoted in: T. Banham, *The sinking of the Lisbon Maru* (HKUP, 2006).

206. J.C. Fallace, Escape Report, 1942, PRO Kew.

207. A.J.W. Evans, Escape Report, 1942, PRO Kew

208. J.C. Fallace, Escape Report, 1942, PRO Kew.

209. *ibid*.

210. Lance Sergeants William Whelan, and Thomas Singleton, Cork; Corporal William Thompson, Killarney; Signalman Henry Fox, Clones; Private Michael O'Connor, Tullamore.

211. Privates John Connolly, Dublin; John Cook, Waterford; William Lawlor, Carlow; Thomas Murphy, Galway; Christopher Samuels, Kildare; Sergeant Patrick Crowley, Cork.

212. Gunners Terence Orr, and Alexander McBride, from Dublin; Henry Couch, Robert Durose, and Jeremiah O'Connell, Cork; John McGivney, Longford; Michael O'Connor, Tullamore; Joseph Gallagher, Leitrim; Michael Kenny, Ardee.

213. T. Banham, *The sinking of the Lisbon Maru* (HKUP, 2006).

214. *ibid*.

215. *ibid*.

216. Daniel Egan, 1st Battalion Middlesex Regiment, 1945, PRO Kew.

217. Evans, Escape Report, 1942 PRO Kew.

218. Report on the sinking ... of the *Lisbon Maru*, Sapper T.S. Taylor RE, 1945, PRO Kew.

219. L.M. Banham, p. 101.

220. Gunner Michael Maher, 1945, PRO Kew.

221. T. Banham, *The sinking of the Lisbon Maru* (HKUP, 2006).

222. *ibid*.

223. PRO Kew.

224. *ibid*.

225. *ibid*.

226. Roly Dean, quoted in, Hugh V. Clarke, *Twilight Liberation* (Allen & Unwin, 1985).

227. *ibid*.

228. Petty Officer Casey, 1945, PRO Kew.

229. T. Banham, *The sinking of the Lisbon Maru* (HKUP, 2006).

230. *ibid*.

231. Emily Hahn, letter to the British Embassy, Washington, 9 March 1944, PRO Kew.

232. T. Banham, *The sinking of the Lisbon Maru* (HKUP 2006).

233. Lance Corporal Michael Walsh, 1945, PRO Kew.

234. Leading Stoker Ashcroft, 1945, PRO Kew.

235. Diary of Captain Duncan, quoted in, Meg Parkes, *Notify Alec Rattray* (Kranji Publications, 2002).

236. A. MacCarthy, *A Doctor's War* (Grubb Street, 2006).

237. *ibid*.

238. Ray Connolly & Bob Wilson, Medical Soldiers, 2/10 Australian Field Ambulance Association, 1985.

239. A. MacCarthy, *A Doctor's War* (Grubb Street, 2006).

240. *ibid*.

241. Anonymous; interview with the author.

242. A. MacCarthy, *A Doctor's War* (Grubb Street, 2006).

243. D. Francis RM, *A Fate worse Than Death*, Force Z Survivors website.

244. *ibid*.

245. *ibid*.

246. N. Tyrer, *Sisters in Arms* (Orion Books, 2008).

247. T. Banham, *The Sinking of the Lisbon Maru* (HKUP, 2006).

248. George Simmonds RM. Interview with the author.

249. *ibid*.

250. *ibid*.

251. Paul Cullen, letter to the author.

252. Harold Lock. Interview with the author.

253. *Daily Telegraph*, 'Revealed: The Most Outrageous US Lawsuits', 20 April 2011.

254. Anonymous. Interview with the author.

255. George Simmonds RM. Interview with the author.

256. Private John Cawley, 1945, PRO Kew.

257. B. MacArthur, *Surviving the Sword* (Time Warner, 2005).

258. Anonymous. Interview with the author.

259. Private Papers of Lieutenant Colonel R. W. Dobbin OBE, 1945, IWM.

260. Lack of space precludes more than a brief outline explanation here. For a fuller explanation Lawrence Rees gives a readable, and compelling, account in *Horrors in the East: The Japanese at War, 1931-1945* (BBC Books, 2001).

261. Western sources estimate a lesser figure of 20,000,000 dead.

262. J. Wyatt, *No Mercy from the Japanese* (Pen & Sword, 2008).

263. Private Jeremiah O'Connor, 1945, PRO Kew.

264. Bernie McGee, letter to the author.

265. Lance Corporal James Hickey, 1945, PRO Kew.

RESEARCH NOTES

The Imperial Japanese Army maintained a system of registration index cards with details of each individual soldier, sailor and airman held in their prison camps. There are around 56,000 British cards. They are now held at the National Archives, in Kew. I went through these cards one by one – a laborious task to put it mildly – and extracted the Irish POWs.

I used the information on the index cards to ascertain who was Irish. Each serviceman had been asked for both their place of origin and their next of kin address. Every card, without exception, has a next of kin address recorded. However, some cards lack a recorded place of origin. This makes deciding nationality more difficult. Where there is a Southern Irish place of origin, and an Irish next of kin address, Irish nationality is clear. Where a POW has an Irish place of origin and a British next of kin address, again Irish nationality appears clear cut. In some instances the place of origin is not recorded, though an Irish next of kin address is given. But with many Irishmen travelling to England for employment, it seems reasonable to assume that, in the context of the time, if a man's next of kin lived in Ireland he was also Irish.

A particular area of concern was the POW record cards for Royal Navy personnel. For whatever reason, origin and next of kin details were often not recorded on their index cards. I suspect that a few Irish citizens serving in the Royal Navy are missing from my research. Overall though, I believe the information I've presented to be accurate. But, if I've wrongly attributed Irish nationality to anyone, or have missed any Irish FEPOWs from the list, I apologise.

The index cards are written in a mixture of Japanese and English. The Japanese script sometimes includes military acronyms, and terminology, that are difficult even for native Japanese speakers to decipher clearly. To make matters even more interesting, the Japanese kanji, or writing, has altered over the last three quarters of a century. Phonetic spellings, and errors, make it obvious that sometimes the English script was written, or typed, by non-native English speakers. Finally, the cause of death is often deliberately misleading – murders and executions tend to be covered up. Other FEPOW documentation, such as records held by the Commonwealth War Graves Commission sometimes offer conflicting dates of death and next of kin.

Analysis of the index cards, and other FEPOW documentation, allows a few interesting insights into the issue of the recruitment of Irish citizens into the British armed services. The received wisdom, when discussing (early twentieth century) Irish enlistment, tells of jobless men, lured from Depression-era dole queues, joining the army as an alternative to starvation. And there is no doubt that many men, in both Ireland and the UK, joined the armed services in the 1920s and 1930s as an alternative to unemployment.

But this doesn't stand scrutiny in the case of the Irish FEPOWs. Yes, some of them enlisted during the 1920s and '30s, but the majority joined from the late 1930s onwards, whilst unemployment was falling and the prospect of war was increasingly obvious. In other words, many joined when alternative work was available, and in the knowledge that they were going to war.

One of the oldest regular soldiers, George Sullivan, born in 1889 at the Curragh, joined the army in 1904 at fifteen years of age. He was a Major in the Royal Army Service Corps, working as a headquarters Staff Officer during the Battle for Singapore. Sullivan went into captivity one week after his fifty-fourth birthday. One of the volunteer reservists, William Magill, from Kerry, had fought in the Boer War and later been wounded in the 1906 Zulu uprising.

A few men enlisted in 1942 during the last desperate weeks of fighting before the fall of Singapore. Frank Smith, from County Donegal, was commissioned into the 2nd Battalion the Malay Regiment on 3 February 1942. At some stage during the following week he was wounded. He was captured at Alexandra Hospital and was one of the casualties who survived the massacre there.

I've (arbitrarily) divided the Irish FEPOWs into four groups. The first group consists of the men who enlisted before 1920; 5 per cent of the POWs. The second group, who enlisted between 1921 and 1930, makes up 10 per cent of the POWs. These were career servicemen, mainly officers and senior non-commissioned officers, men like Company Sergeant Major George Godbold, from Cork. Godbold joined the 1st Battalion of the Leicestershire Regiment in 1926, and served with the battalion in action on the North West Frontier in India.

Though most of the long-term career men were senior in rank, including Lieutenant Colonels, there were a few junior ranks. Gunner William Exley, from Limerick, enlisted as a private soldier in 1924. Trooper Edward Ryan, also from Limerick, signed on with the colours in the same year. The best part of two decades later both men remained private soldiers: long service men toughened by years in the ranks, and service in India, the sort of men easily identified in the works of Rudyard Kipling.

The third group, comprising 31 per cent of the POWs, enlisted between 1931 and 1937. The fourth (and largest) enlistment group, consisting of 54 per cent of the POWs, joined the armed services between 1938 and 1942. Of this last group, over half joined up in 1940, when the war was going very badly for Great Britain.

Attributing reasons for a man's decision to join the armed services is difficult, and generally leads to over-simplification. A sense of adventure remains a generally accepted reason for enlistment in both peace-time and war. A desire to confront Fascism, to do the right thing, can be seen as a more contentious motivator, especially in the context of Irish enlistment in the British armed services during the Second World War. Nonetheless, without wishing to labour the point unduly, the figures speak for themselves and this seems a reasonable premise.

There is little doubt that some of the Irish POWs identified strongly with British interests. Around 10 per cent of the POWs were previously employed in the Civil Service within Hong Kong, Malaya and Singapore. Many of them were members of the reserve and volunteer forces, who were mobilised when Japan invaded Malaya. Others, like Basil O'Connell, serving in uniformed occupations such as the police, were given emergency commissions and attached to regular Army units who made good use of their local knowledge and language skills.

Some of the FEPOWs came from families with a loyalist background. The Japanese Army asked Private Jeremiah O'Connor (from Kerry) for his nationality. He replied Irish, but 'British by birth'.[263] When asked (by the Japanese) for their next of kin address a number of men, like Warrant Officer Robert Wellwood, from 'Queenstown', and Private William Roe, from 'Kingstown', used the pre-independence place names.

Conversely, others were determined that the Japanese should realise that they were Irish citizens and ensured that this was recorded on their POW records. Some came from strongly Irish Republican backgrounds. POW Frank McGee, from Carrick-on-Shannon, was brought up in a house given to his father as part of his pension for services to the Republican cause. After the war, Frank McGee would sometimes be asked why he and his nine brothers enlisted in the British Army. McGee would give the enigmatic, and wonderfully Irish, answer that, 'the English are our enemies and nobody else is allowed to fight them'.[264]

But when going into captivity nationality and national allegiance are fleeting concerns. A soldier's loyalty to his regiment, the men he fights with, transcends issues of nationality. These bonds linking fighting men are powerful and sustaining in adversity. This is why the Japanese often broke up regimental units and separated officers from their men.

Irish POWs had served in virtually every combat regiment and supporting arm of the army, and, in lesser numbers, in the RAF and Royal Navy. Five per cent of the Irish POWs were in the navy, 10 per cent in the air force, and 85 per cent in the army. Over 18 per cent of the Irish POWs serving in the army held commissioned (officer) rank, the most senior being Brigadier Crawford, from County Cork. Twenty per cent of the Royal Navy POWs, and over 23 per cent of the RAF POWs, were also commissioned.

Significant numbers of men, in all three services, held senior non-commissioned ranks, such as Warrant Officer and Sergeant. An even larger number were junior NCOs, Corporals, and Lance Corporals, and their various service equivalents. In other words, a picture emerges of a cohort of men with aptitude and ability achieving well within their chosen career.

Well over half of the (Irish) Army POWs served in combat arms: 33 per cent (of this group) were in the Royal Artillery and 28 per cent in the infantry. But no regiment or corps, from the Royal Army Chaplains' Department, to the Intelligence Corps, lacked an Irish representative. Though one Intelligence Corps soldier, Lance Corporal James Hickey, from Carlow, was wary of receiving special treatment from the Kempeitai, and pretended to be an infantryman when he was captured.[265]

A few Irish POWs served in the Indian Army, which provided both infantry and support troops for the defence of Malaya. Around 10 per cent of the POWs were volunteers – part time soldiers – in local units, such as the Federated Malay States Volunteer Force, and the Hong Kong Volunteer Defence Corps, and so on. This might seem a little odd to readers now. But at the time it would have caused no surprise, as Irish soldiers and civilians served in large numbers throughout the British Empire.

Over half of the POWs came from Dublin and Cork (city and county): 33 per cent and 19 per cent respectively. Only 4 per cent of the POWs came from Limerick and 2 per cent from Galway. The remainder hailed, in varied small percentages, from every other Irish county. Larger population areas inevitably figure more prominently. Aside from that, these figures probably reflect traditional loyalties, attitudes, and recruitment trends, and contain no great surprises.

RECOMMENDED READING

There are hundreds of books written about the Japanese POW camps. Anyone wanting an Irish perspective might do well to start with the following:

John 'Tim' Finnerty's book, *All Hell on the Irrawady*, provides a fascinating account of an Irish career soldier's experience of the Japanese POW camps.

Aidan MacCarthy, in *A Doctor's War*, writes about FEPOW life from the perspective of an Irish doctor serving in the RAF.

In addition:

The Naked Island, by Australian soldier, Russell Braddon, is one of the definitive personal accounts of the Japanese POW camps.

The Sinking of the Lisbon Maru, by Tony Banham, tells the full story of the *Lisbon Maru* disaster.

Moon Over Malaya: A Tale of Argyles and Marines, by Jonathan Moffat and Audrey Holmes McCormick gives a compelling account of the fighting in Malaya.

Printed in Great Britain
by Amazon

34497370R00119